POLITICAL
ANIMALS

POLITICAL ANIMALS

THE SECRET LIFE OF THE POLITICAL PETS OF
WESTMINSTER AND WASHINGTON

PETER CARDWELL

Biteback Publishing

First published in Great Britain in 2025 by
Biteback Publishing Ltd, London
Copyright © Peter Cardwell 2025

Peter Cardwell has asserted his right under the Copyright, Designs and Patents Act 1988 to be identified as the author of this work.

All rights reserved. No part of this publication may be reproduced, stored in a retrieval system or transmitted, in any form or by any means, without the publisher's prior permission in writing.

This book is sold subject to the condition that it shall not, by way of trade or otherwise, be lent, resold, hired out or otherwise circulated without the publisher's prior consent in any form of binding or cover other than that in which it is published and without a similar condition, including this condition, being imposed on the subsequent purchaser.

Every reasonable effort has been made to trace copyright holders of material reproduced in this book, but if any have been inadvertently overlooked the publisher would be glad to hear from them.

ISBN 978-1-785909-900

10 9 8 7 6 5 4 3 2 1

A CIP catalogue record for this book is available from the British Library.

Set in Minion Pro and Futura

Printed and bound in Great Britain by
CPI Group (UK) Ltd, Croydon CR0 4YY

*To my boy Jack – the best cat I could ever wish for
And in memory of Clyde, who left her paw print on my heart*

CONTENTS

Preface ix

PART I: A HISTORY OF POLITICAL ANIMALS 1
Chapter One   A History of British Political Animals   3
Chapter Two   Churchill and His Animals   23
Chapter Three   A History of Presidential Pets   41

**PART II: THE POLITICAL ANIMALS
OF THE WHITE HOUSE** 61
Chapter Four   Post-War Presidential Pets   63
Chapter Five   Contemporary Presidential Pets   89

PART III: THE POLITICAL ANIMALS OF WHITEHALL 103
Chapter Six   Palmerston at the Foreign Office   105
Chapter Seven   Evie and Ossie at the Cabinet Office   123
Chapter Eight   Gladstone at the Treasury   133

**PART IV: THE POLITICAL ANIMALS
OF DOWNING STREET** 141
Chapter Nine   Political Animals at No. 11   143
Chapter Ten   One Prime Minister (and Chancellor) on His Dog: Rishi Sunak on Nova   157

Chapter Eleven	Larry, King of Downing Street	165
Chapter Twelve	One Prime Minister on His Dog: Boris Johnson on Dilyn	193
Chapter Thirteen	One Prime Minister on His Cats: Sir Keir Starmer on Jojo and Prince	203
Chapter Fourteen	One Future (?) Prime Minister on His Dogs: Nigel Farage on Pebble and Baxter	207

PART V: THE POLITICAL ANIMALS OF PARLIAMENT — 211

| Chapter Fifteen | Cronus the Tarantula | 213 |
| Chapter Sixteen | Animals in Parliament | 217 |

PART VI: REFLECTING ON POLITICAL ANIMALS — 233

| Chapter Seventeen | The Pollster and the Psychotherapist | 235 |

Afterword	251
Acknowledgements	257
Index	261

PREFACE

Political life on both sides of the Atlantic has been many things in recent years, but it has seldom been boring. There are few constants; instead, there is a seemingly ever-changing cast of politicians and a revolving door of political debates, referendums, elections and parties. It's been hectic, stressful and often brutal for both those involved and those watching – as I know from personal experience.

But alongside the busyness, there is calm. I've had two jobs in my career: being a special adviser to the UK government, and reporting on it. What no one tells you about politics is that there is an awful lot of hanging about, waiting for things to happen. The Prime Minister has his or her schedule timed to the minute, organised by a small army of people whose job it is to move them from engagement to engagement, maximise every moment and make sure they meet the correct people and there are no exit signs above their head in photographs. But almost everyone else has to wait around for these events to occur to take part in them.

Journalists reporting live from Downing Street may seem in the thick of the action, but the five minutes for which we are on air are often accompanied by fifty-five minutes of that hour waiting for the next 'hit'. There is only so much phoning of sources, checking in with the news desk, reading of Twitter and listening to the cameraman whinge about his break that can be done.

Political life, despite its pace, has many moments of pause. And, as I realised, it also has a lot of paws.

It was on one such slow day back in 2016 I was waiting to broadcast live when I first met Larry the cat. Palmerston, the Foreign Office feline, also came over to say hello. I've always been a huge cat person, so I asked a colleague to take some photos, which I then posted on Twitter.

I quickly realised the snaps of the moggies (and, to a lesser extent, me) had much more of an impact than many of my reports about the humans in Downing Street. 'Look!' people seem to say, 'There are cats! Yes, there's Peter, but mainly there are cats!' It was clearly a rich seam of reporting, so any time I was outside No. 10, I gave a little update on the cats via social media. Many other reporters have done the same, not least Justin Ng, a photojournalist who has become big pals with Larry over the years and never has a packet of treats (specifically Dreamies) far from his reach.

A few days after Sir Keir Starmer was elected Prime Minister in July 2024, I exclusively revealed on Twitter that Jojo, his family's rescue cat, had moved from their home in north London into the flat in Downing Street. I have seldom received such a response: over 1.6 million views and comments from around the world. It brought home that people want to know about politics, yes, but they also want to know about political animals. They're high-profile and much-photographed, but there is always a curiosity about what they may think about their humans and the other politicians who visit their patch. It was once said to me that animals do speak, but only to those humans who know how to listen. I challenge anyone to look at the photograph of

Humphrey the cat and Cherie Blair in the photo section and tell me Humphrey didn't know the score about the controversy around his removal from Downing Street in 1997!

And as someone who loves cats even more than I do politics – for context, my idea of fun as a fifteen-year-old was reading Sir John Major's autobiography – I knew it was time to apply my God-given nerdery to my life's two greatest passions: animals and politics. This book is the result. I know Washington well, having been first an intern at various TV networks and then a professional journalist with the BBC there. I know Westminster even better having been a producer and reporter for a number of stations, most recently as political editor and now presenter on the Talk network. At Talk, we even ran a feature called 'Cat of the Week' on my Saturday shows for 100 editions, in which viewers submitted photographs and videos of their favourite felines. Two of the cats in this book, Evie and Ossie, featured at one stage, as well as the Conservative MP Tom Tugendhat's cat, leading to me referring to him on air as 'Tom Tugendcat'. We eventually extended the remit of the slot and 'Rescue Animal of the Week' was added on Sundays after the inevitable backlash from dog people.

Political Animals is mainly about cats and dogs; however, some arachnophobic readers may wish to skip the short chapter on Cronus the tarantula. Another species features prominently – the main reason for all the cats: the mice! Yes, the kitties are cute, but they *are* also meant to have a job (take note, lazy Larry).

I worked as a special adviser (SpAd) to four Cabinet ministers for three and a half years (2016–20) across four different departments. My time in politics was a busy one, with many reshuffles and a churn of ministers and even Prime Ministers. I wrote a book about it, *The Secret Life of Special Advisers*, published by Biteback. In 2019, I had the pleasure of working with Lucy Frazer KC, who was Prisons Minister in the Ministry of Justice. In all my time working with her, I never saw Lucy rattled. Quite the opposite: I found her diligent, focused and good fun. But there was one issue where Lucy's coping skills deserted her.

Her parliamentary researcher, Timothy Stafford, knew in 2019 that his years of political training, a hard-won degree from Oxford University and his graft and guile in climbing the greasy pole to work for such a high-ranking politician had not been wasted. At around 6 p.m. one evening, Stafford was about to head home when he received a call from his boss summoning him to her main office. 'Timothy,' Frazer reported breathlessly, 'there is a mouse by my handbag, and I need you to be brave!' Stafford rushed to defend his boss, but between them they never found the mouse nor, despite their best efforts, did they get rid of the wider problem of its compatriots in the office. Westminster is full of similar tales.

On numerous occasions, I have been sitting in the House of Commons riverside canteen enjoying their delicious fare and seen mice scurrying along in search of some morsel dropped on the floor. I have, thankfully, never seen a rat, but numerous friends and colleagues have reported those too. The same goes for government offices in Whitehall, where civil servants have been known to sit with their feet slightly off the ground to avoid any encounter with mice.

And it was that desire – both contemporary and historical – to get rid of the rodents that so blight Parliament which has prompted so many politicians to acquire animals, mainly cats.

That said, some politicians, of course, like many people around the world, just love animals and want a dog or cat for their family to care for and to make part of their home.

One of them was Sir Robert Buckland, my boss at the Ministry of Justice when he was Lord Chancellor and Justice Secretary. A few months after I'd left his employment – Boris Johnson's chief enforcer Dominic Cummings had sacked me by that stage – Robert's wife, Sian, lamented the fact that she had a problem getting a cat he would be happy with. Their previous cat, Megan, was a rescue from the welfare charity, Cats Protection. They had tried the local shelters again for the female, grey cat Robert wanted but had had no luck.

'Leave it to me,' I said.

Putting my 'Buckland fixer' hat on once more, I spoke to the Advocacy and Government Relations team at Cats Protection, the part of the charity that campaigns for animal protection legislation. As a lifelong advocate of not buying animals from breeders, I was determined the Bucklands would find a rescue cat. I asked the Cats Protection team if they would like a nice picture of a Cabinet minister and some warm words in a press release (which I would end up mostly authoring) about the charity and the importance of adopting animals. Funnily enough, they welcomed this valuable free publicity.

And thus Tiny, aka Mrs Landingham (after President Bartlet's secretary in the TV series *The West Wing*), became part of the Buckland household in Swindon, where she has thrived and been loved by the family ever since. Job done.

One of the most vilified figures in recent British political history is the aforementioned Dominic Cummings, known best for two things: being Svengali to Boris Johnson and testing his eyes by driving to Barnard Castle during the first Covid lockdown. I always got on with Dominic fine and even after he sacked me, we had a good old chinwag about his historical project on Otto von Bismarck at a wedding. But there is no doubt that Cummings is a hated figure with Bond villian-esque qualities for some. Yet even he is an animal lover.

In a 2025 *Spectator* article, Cummings's wife Mary Wakefield wrote of their new kitten, George:

> Dom is a kind man, but his feelings about the politicians he often works with are not kind. In the pre-George era, his usual monologue, reading the political news of the day, went like this: 'Gah! B******s. Clowns. Idiots.' Just twenty-four hours after George arrived, it took a new turn: 'Gah! B******s. Clowns. Idiots… Oh, hello kitten! What a lovely kitten! What a brave and perfect kitten!'

The cat even made a brief appearance in a Sky News podcast on which Cummings was a guest in May 2025.

Even the Prince of Darkness himself, Peter (now Lord) Mandelson, has always been a dog person. In 2000, the writer Donald Macintyre described how Mandelson, then Northern Ireland Secretary, was speaking to Sinn Féin leader Gerry Adams at Hillsborough Castle when Mandelson's dog, Bobby, came up to the pair with a rubber bullet in his teeth. 'It's my contribution to decommissioning,' Mandelson is reported to have said.

A photograph that sits proudly on display in his official residence is of his late dog Bobby breaking royal protocol by licking

PREFACE

the late Queen's hand. And, more recently, as UK ambassador to the United States, Mandelson was accompanied to Washington by his border collie, Jock.

This book has quite a lot of history in it, but I suspect the current and recent cats and dogs of Westminster and Washington are going to be of most interest to readers. What this book does not really cover is the politics of the last few years, and why should it? There are many books written by much better authors on the internal machinations, the changes and battles of politics. I'll leave it to the experts to tell you what really occurred in the rooms where it happened; I'm going to tell you about some players who observe major events, never leak stories and can humanise even the most loathed figures in Washington and Westminster.

There are so many intriguing, fun and outrageous stories about animals in politics. My plan is to take you by the hand – or even the paw – and lead you behind the black door of Downing Street and inside the White House to hear from key people, some of whom have never given interviews before, about the wonderful world of our furry friends, the political animals of Westminster and Washington.

Peter Cardwell
London
July 2025
#AdoptDontShop

PART I

A HISTORY OF POLITICAL ANIMALS

CHAPTER ONE

A HISTORY OF BRITISH POLITICAL ANIMALS

In Ancient Egypt, cats were worshipped as gods. The Chinese looked to dogs for guidance in antiquity. The reign of Roman Emperor Caligula, who ruled from AD 37 to AD 41, can be described as eccentric at best and at worst, unhinged and cruel. Animals played a part in his mercurial leadership. He once threatened to make his horse, Incitatus, a consul – one of the highest Roman political offices. Some historians see this as a sign of Caligula's madness; others view it as a rebuke to the senators of Rome in implying that a horse could do a better job than they.

In England, cats have quite literally been at the seat of power since the time of Cardinal Wolsey. Wolsey was Lord Chancellor between 1515 and 1529, during the reign of King Henry VIII. Today, a bronze statue of Wolsey in his home town of Ipswich, located in the east of England, features a familiar face peering out from behind his robes – the four-legged su-purr-visor of all that went on in the Tudor court.

Historian Claire Ridgway notes that cats were not a popular pet at the time due to their association with the Devil and witchcraft. It is an urban myth that Pope Innocent VIII decreed cats as unholy creatures in 1484 and that they should be torched alongside the witches that owned them. When witches were burned at the stake, it was often said that a black cat leapt out of the flames.

Nonetheless, Wolsey clearly held his cat dear, and though it was the first pet ever recorded at the centre of government, it was likely animals, and cats in particular, had been part of politics in Britain for many years before.

Sir Richard Whittington (1354–1423), for example, is well known for his own furry companion through the popular folk tale of Dick Whittington and his cat. The story goes that Dick, a penniless orphan, became Lord Mayor of London in the fifteenth century. He began life as a servant and his master asked each of his employees to surrender their most valued item to a sea captain who would go abroad and sell that item. Dick was of course reluctant to part with his cat. But the sacrifice worked when the King of Barbary, whose palace was overrun with mice, bought the cat for a large sum of money. With his fortunes on the rise, Dick had the means to become Lord Mayor of London.

There is a statue of his famous cat in Highgate Hill in London and, while there is no substantive evidence that the real Dick Whittington was poor, an orphan or even had a cat, the tale is told in pantomimes and story times across the United Kingdom and beyond to this day. Oh yes it is!

In more recent history, in Victorian England, Tom the cat lived at Downing Street from around 1878 to 1892 during the periods of office of Benjamin Disraeli, William Ewart Gladstone and Robert Gascoyne-Cecil. A number of senior politicians were known to pet Tom, not least Gladstone himself. Sadly, Tom, according to the *Manchester Evening News* on 22 January 1892, was 'to the general grief of the inhabitants in the vicinity ... set upon by two bull terriers and, after a brave fight, was killed.'

Dr Patrick Little, senior research fellow at the History of

Parliament project, points out that leaders such as Oliver Cromwell in the seventeenth century used the image of the 'country squire' to bolster, or even spin, their social origins. Cromwell was really more farmer than squire: the historian Lady Antonia Fraser writes of Cromwell in St Ives in the early 1630s as 'farming his cattle, bringing up his family, and showing himself a solid local man'. His affinity with animals was used to portray him as a man of the people.

Many British politicians throughout the ages have used animals to soften their image with the public – or, in Cromwell's case, create it. Certainly, in the political world from which many feel excluded, the ordinariness and relatability of animals has provided a way for people to engage with politics. A prime contemporary example of this is Larry the Downing Street cat (fear not, he has a chapter all to himself later) who has hit the headlines many times, but even over a century ago, there was great press – and public – interest in the cats of Westminster.

In January 1903, during Arthur Balfour's premiership, the *Dundee Evening Telegraph* ran the headline 'Lost! The Downing Street Cat' and asked if anyone had seen Topsy. She had clashed with the Chancellor of the Exchequer's cat Tom, having beaten him 'in the best of three rounds'. Topsy 'was a general favourite … a good cat of her claws', but she disappeared after the fight, leaving Balfour bereft and Tom 'inconsolable' too.

In 1907, the society magazine *Tatler* featured a detailed article on 'Cats in Office: Mieous from Whitehall', which explained the difference between the two types of resident feline.

The office cat, said *Tatler*, 'seldom has any *locus standi* [legal standing] and lives on charity all year round' whereas the official cat 'is a recognised member of the community and has a fixed allowance for food and other necessities'. As part of the article, *Tatler* photographed seven of these cats in and around government buildings: Tommy Liza the Privy Council cat, Toby the Home Office cat, Joe the Board of Education cat, Tits and Tats the Mansion House cats, Trillie Williams the War Office cat and Duke, the Paymaster General's cat.

Tommy Liza was 'always in disgrace in spite of his sixteen years', and his 'favourite resting place' was the chair of the Marquess of Crewe, Lord President of the Council from 1915 to 1916. Toby was 'the Home Office cat, eleven years old and a sufferer from chronic asthma'. Joe was a 'terror to the pigeons living nearby'. Tits and Tats, reported *Tatler*, were 'lively youngsters' who 'evinced a great dread of the camera and, like the small infant, [had] to be held in position to have their photograph taken'. Trillie Williams was nine years old, continually sleepy and had a 'preference for the cook's bed'. Last came Duke, the Paymaster General's cat, who was a present from the Duke of Wellington, hence his name, and was very energetic.

There weren't just cats – or indeed dogs – living in Downing Street at this time. Sir William Harcourt kept a canary at No. 11, the official residence of the Chancellor of the Exchequer, while he held the title between 1892 and 1895. According to the *Oxford Chronicle and Reading Gazette*, the bird 'escaped a few years before the General Election in 1895' but 'was recaptured soon after' its bid for freedom. Prime Minister David Lloyd George's dog went missing in 1918, with the *Croydon Times* reporting his Welsh terrier Cymro had been 'lost at Sutton on 19 July whilst Mr Lloyd George was addressing a War Weapons Campaign meeting'. According to the *Daily Mirror* eleven days later, a resident of Redhill claimed the £5 reward having found the dog 'wandering around' and temporarily given him a home. Frilly was the British War Office cat some time around 1909. When he died, the office staff had a whip-round to pay for him to be stuffed, and he was displayed in the Imperial War Museum's exhibition 'Animals' War' in 2017.

'If you look at the records, there is very much an idea that in the 1920s, these are working animals,' Christopher Day, author of *Larry the Chief Mouser: And Other Official Cats*, told *Politico* in 2023. 'They were being paid for out of public funding – which is not the case now – and they were expected to earn their keep.'

Not all the animals were politicians' pets, however. On 8 June 1923, a dog made its presence felt to a House of Commons committee discussing street betting. The *Daily Herald* reported how a black and white terrier 'quietly strayed into the room in Westminster Palace, and, unobtrusively stalking about the tables, made a mute appeal to members … he was stroked and petted by a number of the MPs'.

As war loomed in 1939, Bob the Downing Street cat was thought to be a sign of good luck. He had been spotted during the signing of the Munich Agreement the year before and was seen again just days before the outbreak of the Second World War. The *Dundee Courier* wrote:

> The famous black cat which has given a homely touch in Downing Street in times of international crisis reappeared yesterday afternoon. It walked nonchalantly up the street, and as it reached the door of No. 10 there was a cheer by

the onlookers. When photographers rushed forward the cat turned round and scampered out of sight.

By the time Bob died in August 1943, he had become one of the most photographed cats in the world.

Churchill first became Prime Minister in 1940. He recognised, as have many who have worked in the aged buildings of Whitehall and Westminster, that rodent infestations can be dealt with by employing cats. However, Churchill didn't limit himself to cats – more on that in Chapter Two.

While there were clear indicators of official versus unofficial cats in Whitehall, it appears the role of chief mouser of the United Kingdom dates back to at least 1924. The first to take on this role was a marmalade cat who had two names: Smokey and Rufus of England. The Chancellor of the day, Philip Snowden, had a reputation for being parsimonious; nevertheless, upon noticing a rather thin-looking Smokey/Rufus one day, decided to increase the cat's rations by half. But in order for this to happen, a bill had to be passed in Parliament first. This led to the cat acquiring yet another name: Treasury Bill. Treasury Bill was a formidable mouser and ratter and was known to bring 'trophies' to his boss. When the cat realised that these thoughtful gifts were being thrown into rubbish bins, he started to leave the dead mice neatly laid out beside the bins for the cleaners. A considerate feline.

In 1936, the Cabinet Office argued that Jumbo, their resident mouser, deserved an allowance. When he died eight years later, the world was at war and men needed at the front, so one Cabinet Office wag suggested that Jumbo's successor should be female, given that women were doing so many of the jobs that men had done previously.

Historians disagree on which was the first official government cat, but we do know that Peter lived in the Home Office from 1929 to 1946. His upkeep was funded by voluntary contributions from civil servants, as is the case for the cats of Whitehall today. He was so loved, and indeed spoiled, that he was not particularly good at the serious business of actually chasing mice. (It appears the pattern started early on this point – Larry, we're looking at you.) To tackle the issue, the Home Office asked the Treasury for a formal food budget to limit Peter's overindulgence, get him into shape and to allow him to turn his paws to the role which was supposedly his raison d'être. One penny a week was agreed for Peter's upkeep.

Peter performed his duties well under this new regime. Indeed, when a section of the Home Office moved to Bournemouth during the Second World War, Peter was so missed that staff there applied for an allowance to keep two cats. They penned a poem in February 1941 to put forward their intriguing suggestion:

> Establishments approval seek
> To spend say one and six per week
> For beverage and food (ersatz)
> On each of Bournemouth's office cats.
> This situation is complex
> Because we do not know their sex.
> To pay for grub we hesitate,
> For 'pussies' who may propagate.
> But if they'll give a guarantee

> They won't produce a family
> Of little 'mousers' of their ilk,
> We'll meet the cost of food and milk.

A senior civil servant reviewing the proposal wrote to his superiors: 'Subject to the proviso in the third stanza, I think approval should be given.' Alas, in 1946, at the age of seventeen, Peter was put to sleep.

His successor was Peter II, a two-month-old male kitten. But the sequel sadly did not last as long as the original as Peter II was tragically run over on Whitehall in June 1947. Three days later, police constable N. Hawe wrote to the Office Keeper, Mr McMillin:

> Sir,
> At 3.15 a.m. on 21 June 1947 the P.C. on duty outside the Home Office brought to the door 'Peter' (H.O. Cat), which, just previously when crossing the road to the Cenotaph, was run over by a motorcar driven by Mr. R. B. BISGOOD 8. Welbeck Street. W1.
> The cat received injury to the head, right shoulder and a lacerated jaw; at 3.20 a.m. I telephoned the Night Service, R.S.P.C.A. 105 Jermyn Street. (Whi. 7177.), at 3.35 a.m. their representative attended. After a careful examination he advised that it was for the best to have him put to sleep; to which I, rather reluctantly, agreed. Mr. Bisgood gave two shillings for the services rendered, receipt attached.
> N. Hawe P.C. 365.

Just two months later, a successor to Peter II was found, with the highly original name Peter III. He joined the Home Office on

27 August 1947. Peter III appeared on the BBC in 1958 and was pictured in newspapers and magazines, including the October 1962 issue of *Woman's Realm*. His rations were controversial, too, but for a different reason: many members of the animal-loving public believed them to be meagre. One even wrote to the Home Office and received the following reply:

> The mice which Peter is employed to catch are not mere 'perks'; they are intended to be, and should be, his staple food … Peter's emoluments [salary] are not designed to keep him in food: if they were, they would also keep him in idleness.

Peter III received much fan mail throughout his life, and many messages of condolence were sent to the Home Office when he was put to sleep on 9 March 1964. One letter came from the New York Transit Authority's 'Etti-Cat', a moggy whose job was to promote courtesy on the city's subway. Many letters also came from Italy where, for some reason, Peter III was particularly loved and missed. To mark his passing, Home Office staff raised money to pay for a headstone at the People's Dispensary for Sick Animals pet cemetery in Ilford, Essex.

Presumably because calling his successor Peter IV would have been too predictable, the name was feminised to Peta. She was a Manx cat and gift from the lieutenant governor of the Isle of Man. Day describes Peta in his book as 'inordinately fat and lazy because she'd been fed so many treats'. According to Day and Marianne Whitworth in a National Archive blog post, Peta once got into a fight with Nemo, Harold Wilson's male point Siamese and, in attempting to break up the cats, Mary Wilson, the Prime Minister's wife, suffered a cut and reportedly had to cancel a dinner with the Italian Prime Minister when the wound turned septic.

Nemo moved into Downing Street after Wilson's election and would accompany the family on their annual holiday to the Scilly Isles, off the south-west coast of Cornwall. They were also joined by Paddy, the Wilsons' golden Labrador. A present from George Wigg, the paymaster-general, Paddy was initially sent to Wilson's sister's home in Cornwall with instructions that the dog take an obedience course.

The writer Isabel Wolff recalled upon Wilson's death in 1995 that he might well have died decades earlier in the Scilly Isles had it not been for a fortunate encounter with her family. In 1973, the Wolffs were on their annual holiday when Isabel heard faint cries of distress coming from the water. She found a golden Labrador, presumably belonging to the man shouting, tied up near the boats on the shore. Her father and brothers raced to the rescue, heaving him onboard and rowing back to shore.

The grateful man explained that he had slipped out of his rubber dinghy trying to get into the launch but hadn't been able to pull himself back out of the water. He had been there for at least half an hour. Wolff's father soon realised that he had rescued none other than former Prime Minister Harold Wilson. Wilson was, understandably, embarrassed. He slowly walked off with Paddy, having asked the family to spare his blushes publicly. However, the press got the story about a month later, with headlines including 'Wilson Rescued in Sea Drama', 'Wilson Snatched From Drowning', 'Scilly Secret Floats to the Surface' and, from the *Daily Mirror*, '"My Dog Tipped Me In"'. In her account, Isabel Wolff continues:

Mr Wilson's press secretary, Joe Haines, had blamed Paddy. There was even a photo of the dog captioned 'The Culprit'! One could see the need for damage-limitation – after all, it was embarrassing for Wilson, not least because Edward Heath was a serious yachtsman – but Paddy, I know for sure, was innocent … Joe Haines made light of the incident. Wilson, he claimed, was in 'no danger' and 'could have swum to the beach' but was 'waiting for a friend to turn up'.

Harold Wilson would almost certainly have died. He was fifty-seven, he was overweight, he'd been in the freezing water for more than half an hour and his arms were giving out. The Atlantic currents were very strong, there was no one around, and it was only by the slimmest chance that my father heard his cries. He knew he had had an extremely close shave, but had obviously been persuaded to let the dog take the blame and play down the incident.

In 1974, Wilberforce the cat, dubbed 'the best mouser in Britain', arrived at Downing Street from the RSPCA (Royal Society for the Prevention of Cruelty to Animals). He served four Prime Ministers during the 'pendulum politics' of the 1970s, starting with Wilson's second premiership through to Thatcher's period of office in the 1980s. Thatcher once brought him a tin of sardines from a visit to Moscow, according to her press secretary Sir Bernard Ingham. Sir Bernard, an asthmatic, was allergic to cats and did his best to avoid Wilberforce, but it was easier said than done. 'Bloody Wilberforce used to sit under my desk and I would have a fit of sneezing,' he recalled. 'I hate cats.'

Wilberforce also made an appearance during the general

election coverage in 1983, when he was held by presenter Esther Rantzen and introduced to BBC viewers. Wilberforce left Downing Street in 1986 after thirteen years of loyal service. He went to live in the country with a retired No. 10 caretaker and he died in his sleep on 19 May 1988.

Away from Downing Street, but still with significant ramifications across Westminster, the 1970s saw a very British scandal unfold in the form of the infamous Jeremy Thorpe affair. Thorpe, in part, was brought down by a dog – a Great Dane named Rinka. The Liberal leader's case became world famous after he and three co-defendants stood trial at the Old Bailey in 1979 for the attempted murder of Norman Scott. Scott was a troubled young man with whom Thorpe had begun an affair before homosexuality was decriminalised. Despite Thorpe's attempts to pay Scott off, Scott threatened to go public about their affair, posing a danger to Thorpe and the rising popularity of his party.

The situation spiralled, and a would-be hitman called Andrew Newton was sent after Scott. Newton made several attempts to lure Scott out before eventually persuading him to meet on Exmoor just to talk. Newton objected to Rinka tagging along as he was, ironically, rather scared of dogs. Tragically, Rinka came anyway. What happened next became a stain from which Thorpe's career would not recover. When the party got to a deserted stretch of the road, Newton took out a gun and shot Rinka in the head, before turning to Scott, saying, chillingly, 'It's your turn now.' However, the second shot failed and, having botched the murder, Newton drove away at speed, leaving Scott with his dying dog. The *West Somerset Free Press* reported the Rinka tragedy under the headline: 'The Great Dane Mystery: Dog-in-a-Fog Case Baffles Police'.

Thorpe was charged alongside three others with conspiracy to murder Norman Scott, and though he was later acquitted, his reputation was ruined. Thorpe resigned as leader of the Liberal Party and lost his seat in the 1979 general election. Auberon Waugh stood against him in his North Devon seat, running as the candidate for the Dog Lovers' Party, receiving seventy-nine votes.

Of course not all stories involving political animals are nearly as dramatic. Another tale emerged in September 1995, this time not at Downing Street, but John Major's constituency home in Huntingdonshire. Although a tough time politically for Major, he made his rival party leaders Tony Blair and Paddy Ashdown laugh uproariously during the Victory in Japan Day commemorations when recounting how a goldfish in his pond needed medical attention after becoming sunburned. The fish, reported the *Aberdeen Press & Journal*, 'was taken from its watery living quarters and an attempt was made to revive it – using sun cream'. It is not known whether the fish survived.

Humphrey the cat came to Downing Street in 1989 and faithfully served both the Thatcher and Major administrations before leaving under something of a cloud during Tony Blair's first year. Like Bob, the 'omen of good luck' about fifty years earlier, Humphrey arrived as a stray, having been originally found wandering the streets by a Cabinet Office civil servant a few months after the death of the previous mouser, Wilberforce. He was named after Sir Humphrey Appleby, Nigel Hawthorne's fictional Permanent Secretary in the TV comedies *Yes, Minister* and *Yes, Prime Minister*. The Cabinet Office's previous pest controller charged £4,000 per annum. At just £100 a year, Humphrey was much more economical. In 1993, a Cabinet Office memo told civil servants that Humphrey had a kidney complaint. 'As well as being treated by a vet he has been placed on a controlled diet and is not to eat anything other than the prescribed food,' the Cabinet Office memo read. 'Staff are therefore asked that, for his own good, he is not fed any treats or titbits.' An earlier memo, prepared by the accommodation officer at the Cabinet Office at 70 Whitehall, explained:

> He tends to eat little and often – no doubt because he knows he can always get food whenever he wants ... He is a workaholic who spends nearly all his time at the office, has no criminal record, does not socialise a great deal or go to many parties and has not been involved in any sex or drugs scandals that we know of.

Humphrey also technically 'belonged' to the Cabinet Office rather than the neighbouring No. 10, but as any owner will tell you, cats don't usually answer to anyone other than themselves. His food budget came out of the Cabinet Office's funds, yet he was frequently found on Downing Street. One of his favourite ways to spend his time was to sit on top of the hot air vent just outside the front door of No. 10, something Larry still does.

In spring 1994, Humphrey was accused of the murder of four robin chicks near the Prime Minister's Office. However, the cat had his defenders, not least one civil servant who argued in a memo that Humphrey 'could not have caught anything even if it had been roast duck with orange sauce presented to him on a plate'. They insisted that the four robins in the window box had perished via other means: 'This was a libellous allegation and was completely unfounded. This was at a time when Humphrey, a gentle-natured cat, had been ill with kidney trouble and sleeping for most of the day.'

A London newspaper requested an interview with Humphrey about the robin controversy but they were denied: 'Unfortunately as Humphrey is a civil servant he is bound by civil service rules and cannot talk to the press about his position.' Prime Minister John Major soon exonerated Humphrey, stating to reporters, 'I am afraid Humphrey has been falsely accused.' In 2006, George Jones, the *Daily Telegraph* journalist who wrote the story, admitted that he had made it up. Jones had indeed been shown the dead robins by Major on a visit to Downing Street, but there was no evidence to suggest that it was Humphrey who had caused their death. Yet, proving that mud sticks, later that year Humphrey was accused of having 'savaged' a duck in the nearby St James's Park.

Much like Larry, Humphrey was described as a very relaxed, laid-back cat, unperturbed by the great matters of state around him or the famous people, flashbulbs of photographers and general fuss that occurs at Downing Street. On one occasion, King Hussein of Jordan was kept waiting while a police officer removed Humphrey from the red carpet. When American President Bill Clinton came to visit, Humphrey felt the need to go over and investigate the presidential Cadillac and came close to being run over in the process.

Despite, or perhaps because of, these news-grabbing mishaps, a cat food company requested that Humphrey star in its adverts but, according to the *Daily Record*, was told 'paws off'. Apparently, as Humphrey was a civil servant, it would be against his contract to take advertising work. His likeness, however, did appear on the small screen, satirised in the TV comedy series *Spitting Image* as a cat who criticised Sir John Major. However, there is no evidence to suggest Humphrey and Major ever got on anything other than very well.

In June 1995 Humphrey performed a vanishing act, only returning some months later. No. 10 had kept his disappearance quiet until a journalist on *The Times*, Sheila Gunn, told a member of staff there that her own cat had died. Conversation then turned to the missing Humphrey and the story was made public. Finally, in September, the *Daily Mirror* reported that 'Humphrey the Downing Street cat has been found safe three months after disappearing'. There were some red faces at *The Times* newspaper, which had already printed his obituary. It transpired that a policeman at the Royal Army Medical College, about a mile from Downing Street, had found Humphrey, thought he was a stray, took him in and called him PC, short for 'Patrol Cat.' Eventually, the policeman recognised Humphrey's photo and the cat was returned to his Downing Street home.

Safely back in No. 10, Humphrey issued a statement via the civil service: 'I have had a wonderful holiday at the Royal Army Medical College, but it is nice to be back and I am looking forward to the new parliamentary session.' He even received a message of support from Socks, America's 'First Cat', welcoming him back. Socks, himself a popular political animal, belonged to the Clintons and ruled the roost at the White House.

This was not the only time that Humphrey found a new home, however. He was quite innocently catnapped by a member of the public in 1997. A German travel agent, Hanni Velden, spotted

Humphrey wandering around St James's Park, something he did fairly often. Velden mistakenly thought Humphrey was a stray, picked him up and brought him to her flat in Lambeth, south London. She subsequently took him to the vet for a check-up whereupon someone else recognised Humphrey. The Cabinet Office was given a call to check whether he was missing, they confirmed that he was and Humphrey was returned.

But trouble lay ahead. Later that same year, Humphrey was 'retired' shortly after Tony Blair became Prime Minister and his family moved into Downing Street. Initial reports suggested that Cherie Blair, the Prime Minister's wife, was either allergic to cats or believed them to be unhygienic. This was later revealed to have been an invention of a press adviser to Major. 'One of the first things the children wanted to see when they moved into No. 11 was Humphrey,' a spokesman said at the time, denying the allegations. 'Cherie and her sister had both a cat and a dog when they were growing up. This is Humphrey's home and, as far as the Blairs are concerned, it will remain his home.' Curiously for a statement released to the media under the watch of communications director Alastair Campbell at No. 10, the latter part didn't prove to be fully factual. The Press Association was invited to take a photo of Cherie Blair with Humphrey in her arms, proving just how much they truly loved one another; neither appeared particularly happy to be there (see photo section). Tony Blair later admitted it was the biggest political crisis of his first year as Prime Minister.

But Humphrey's retirement was more about his advancing years than any conspiracy to get rid of him by Mrs Blair, Campbell or anyone else, however convenient it was for them to be portrayed as pantomime villains of the piece. In early November 1997, Humphrey's primary carer, a civil servant called Jonathan Rees who worked in the No. 10 Policy Unit, wrote a memo suggesting that the ageing cat should be allowed to retire to a 'stable home environment where he can be looked after properly'. A vet agreed, especially as Humphrey's kidney complaint had persisted and he had lost interest in food.

So, on 13 November, Humphrey left Downing Street and moved in with an older couple in the London suburbs, one of them a Cabinet Office civil servant. His departure was only announced the following day, in case there was an attempt to catnap him. The Conservatives were quick to point out that Humphrey had happily lived in Downing Street for eight years under their government, but New Labour meant a new home for Humphrey. Animal rights supporter and outspoken Conservative MP Alan Clark said, 'Humphrey is now a missing person. Unless I hear from him or he makes a public appearance, I suspect he has been shot.' Further mischievous claims against Cherie Blair alleged that Humphrey had been put down on her orders.

While the Prime Minister's wife was certainly unfairly vilified in some regards when it came to Humphrey, Labour MP Chris Mullin revealed in his diaries, published in 2009, that she did indeed feel at least some antipathy towards the cat. Shortly after her infamous photocall with Humphrey, Mullin spoke to Mrs Blair: 'I mentioned that I had seen Humphrey the cat on my visit to No. 10 yesterday. "Give him a kick from me," she said. So the rumours are true.'

Further political mischief was made by the Conservatives' Constitutional Affairs spokesman Nigel Evans MP, who linked Humphrey's exit to the controversy over a donation made to

Labour by Formula One chief executive Bernie Ecclestone (the sport was later exempted from a ban on tobacco advertising). Said Evans:

> Humphrey clearly can't stand the stench of hypocrisy which reeks from Downing Street after the 'donations for exemptions' affair, Humphrey is voting with his paws to leave the Downing Street lair. After eight happy years under a Conservative government he could only take six months of Labour before he lost interest in living.
>
> Perhaps, like all other groups who have suffered from Labour's broken promises, he didn't get the loving attention he was promised in May from the new occupants of No. 10.

Eleven days after Humphrey left Downing Street a group of journalists was taken to a secret location, which may have been his new home, to prove that he was alive and well, and that he had even put on some weight. The pictures of a happy, healthy Humphrey were published in the papers the next day.

After Humphrey left, the Downing Street spin machine claimed that 'a new puss has been interviewed and will soon replace Humphrey on Downing Street rodent duty'. But it never happened under the Blair administration.

The cat remained happily in retirement until March 2006, when a spokesman for Tony Blair informed the press that Humphrey had died at the age of eighteen, which is a good age for a male cat. Paying tribute, Conservative MP Roger Gale, a frequent visitor to 10 Downing Street during the Thatcher and Major years, said:

Humphrey was often curled up on the doorkeeper's chair and a very reassuring presence to those entering No. 10 on business. We were sad when Humphrey was 'retired' with the arrival of the Blairs. Humphrey clearly had a much loved and comfortable old age. We were all sorry to learn, today, of his death, and we shall all remember the Downing Street cat with great affection.

CHAPTER TWO

CHURCHILL AND HIS ANIMALS

If any UK Prime Minister was an animal lover, it was Winston Churchill. He did much to help animals' cause, both directly and indirectly, at a time when they had far fewer protections than today. As much of the writing on him reveals, Churchill's interest in the animal kingdom permeated all aspects of his life, from his politics and how he wrote to his speeches and how he treated those around him. Even the smallest species was regarded with respect; he saved earthworms while playing golf and once asked an American general to open a window so he could release a ladybird that had landed on his sleeve. Churchill also took in numerous strays, never abandoning them even if they were ill or badly behaved.

Churchill was an equestrian for much of his life. He rode his first pony, Rob Roy, from the age of seven. Later, Churchill led the lancers in Britain's last cavalry charge at the Battle of Omdurman. He owned and bred prize-winning horses, the first and most famous being Colonist II in 1949.

Churchill was born into an era of huge wealth inequality, when it was almost impossible to truly look after an animal as a pet unless one had the means to do so. He had such means; many others who did not understandably tended to see animals as food or to assist in agricultural work or transportation. His love of animals was so well known that, during the war, his secretary had to turn down numerous offers of cats from both allies and voters. This aspect of his personality has long since faded from the public consciousness, supplanted by other Churchill leitmotifs such as his 'bulldog' image and his stoicism in the face of war.

Later in life, Churchill 'collected' animals. He tended to decide on a whim that he would like to have a new type of animal and when it became too large or difficult, it was transferred to London Zoo. The zoo was glad to receive the animals, finding that visitor numbers increased as a result. Amongst those who made the journey were albino kangaroos Digger (see photo section) and Matilda; a lion, Rota; and Churchill's collection of tropical fish. Churchill would visit his animals as a form of relaxation. In his book *Churchill's Bestiary*, Piers Brendon writes that Churchill had so many pets over the course of his life that he could probably have opened his own zoo, or at least a petting zoo. Churchill had a childish fascination with carnivals, fairs, zoos and circuses. Brendon suggests that Churchill's love of Rudyard Kipling was the inspiration for his famous 'We shall fight on the beaches' speech – in much the same way, the seals in *The Jungle Book* 'fought in the breakers, they fought on the sand, and they fought on the smooth-worn basalt rocks of the nurseries'.

Churchill was ahead of his time in terms of his respect for animals and their rights. That said, he certainly fitted the stereotype of the rich safari hunter and had killed animals for sport, but he fundamentally understood animals much more in the way we do today. Churchill was equally an enthusiastic foxhunter and someone who called foxes his 'friends' and kept them as pets. He couldn't resist any animal and his staff, especially on his estate, ended up caring for them all. Churchill once remarked that, without his staff's help, he 'might literally be petted to death'.

Not all of them were exotic animals. Churchill cherished his bulldog Dodo, his wartime cat Nelson and his much-loved poodle Rufus. Over the decades, dozens of creatures made their home at Chartwell from cows to cats, pheasants, swans and even butterflies. But Churchill had a particular fondness, even respect, for his prized Middle White pigs. He famously stated in 1952, 'Dogs look up to you, cats look down on you. Give me a pig! He looks you in the eye and treats you as an equal.'

In a 1935 letter to his wife Clementine, while she was on a cruise in the South Pacific, Churchill brought her up to date on the latest exploits of Chartwell's menagerie. Mary Soames, the youngest of Churchill's children, included the letter in *Winston and Clementine: The Personal Letters of the Churchills*: 'The cat treats me well very graciously and always wishes to sleep on my bed (which I resent). When I dine alone, and only then, she awaits me on the table.'

Even after his stroke in 1953, Clementine remarked, 'The old lion could still issue from his den and, when he did so, his growl was as frightening as ever.' He was famously nicknamed the British Bulldog, encapsulating the fighting spirit of the nation during the Second World War, an image which has endured. But he also had his own 'black dog' as he termed it, a reference to his fight with the plague of depression. At the time, the phrase typically just referred to bad moods, although some historians believe that Churchill was battling stronger distress.

In 1927, Churchill was given a pair of black swans by Sir Philip Sassoon, which were kept in the lake at Chartwell. Churchill was impressed by their stature and grace, writing to Sassoon that they 'sing to one another beautifully, and dance minuets with their necks'. Soon after their arrival, a wire fence was erected around the upper lake to protect them from his mute swan, Jupiter, whom Churchill described as 'irate'. The number of swans kept by Churchill fluctuated and they were sometimes difficult to keep alive due to predators. As time passed, the Australian government continued to give Churchill replacement swans, a symbol of the Anglo-Australian bond and a gesture genuinely welcomed by Churchill. One of the last letters signed by Churchill before his death was a letter to Australian Prime Minister Robert Menzies, dated June 1964, thanking him for sending a new pair of swans.

Another relatively unusual interest of Churchill's was his fascination with insects, particularly butterflies. As a boy he was renowned as a 'bug-hunter' and an amateur collector, and in the aftermath of the Second World War he bred them at Chartwell, helped by an expert entomologist; 500 half-grown peacock caterpillars were once delivered to the estate. As Brendon points out, the names of butterfly species appealed greatly to Churchill: elephant hawk-moths, scarlet tigers, white admirals, speckled woods and painted ladies.

Chartwell was fundamental to Churchill's love of animals, with its open space and facilities allowing him to indulge his passion. He bought the Kent estate in 1922 early in his career when he was a successful government minister, MP and author. Like many of the upper classes in the post-war years, Churchill struggled with the financial demands of a large estate. Churchill did a deal through which Chartwell became a National Trust property but he was granted a life tenancy, which Clementine eventually gave up in 1966.

Part of the agreement stipulated there would always be an orange cat with a white bib and four white socks named Jock in residence. Why? Because the original Jock – an eighty-eighth birthday present to Churchill from his private secretary Sir John 'Jock' Colville, after whom the cat was named – was such a great friend to Churchill at Chartwell. He was a true comfort to Churchill in his final years and even took pride of place, sat on his master's knee, in the photographs of the wedding of Churchill's grandson.

The tradition of a Jock at Chartwell endures to this day. Jock VII, a six-month-old RSPCA rescue kitten, arrived at Chartwell in May 2020 and, much like his predecessors, quickly became head honcho. Having started life in difficult conditions – alongside dozens of other cats rescued with him – his rags-to-riches tale is now complete, with the National Trust reporting that Jock VII enjoys 'investigating what the gardeners are up to and playing down in the long grasses of the orchard. He also likes lots of cuddles on the sofa after an eventful day.' Having a Jock at Chartwell in perpetuity certainly cements Churchill's legacy as an animal lover committed to helping them find good homes. The original Jock was allowed to sleep on the same bed as Churchill – a privilege that the Chartwell Jocks enjoy to this day.

As war raged across Europe in 1941, with the Allies on the back foot having suffered a number of naval defeats, Churchill, his private secretary Colville and Tango the cat had lunch together. In his book, Brendon cites Colville's recollection of Tango being seated in his own chair next to Churchill, who 'kept up a running conversation with the cat, cleaning its eyes with a napkin, offering it mutton and expressing regret that it could not have cream in wartime'. Sadly Tango died a year later, about the same time as the fall of Tobruk, so Colville and other advisers decided to withhold the news about Tango's passing from Churchill until the war situation began to look up.

To the general public, though, it was a large grey cat called Nelson who was most associated with Prime Minister Churchill during the war. American war correspondent Quentin Reynolds, author of *All About Winston Churchill*, noted his subject's love of animals and of Nelson in particular. 'Nelson is the bravest cat I ever knew,' Churchill once said. 'I once saw him chase a huge dog out of the Admiralty. I decided to adopt him and name him after our great Admiral.' Reynolds writes about having dinner with the then Prime Minister: 'Churchill scarcely mentioned the war. Our first course was smoked salmon and twice, when Mrs Churchill was not looking, the Prime Minister sneaked pieces of salmon to Nelson.'

With a self-confidence that Larry would be proud of, Nelson was just a few moments into his new home at No. 10 before he gave chase to and asserted his authority over Neville Chamberlain's cat, who was known derogatorily as the 'Munich Mouser' after the previous Prime Minister's deal that promised – but did not deliver – 'peace in our time'.

Nelson was Churchill's 'hot water bottle', according to Brendon, and was, like many of his pets, extremely spoiled. Even during wartime rationing, when most food was scarce, the cat was treated to pheasant, cream and smoked salmon. Nelson was even included in the family's evacuation plans should Downing Street be attacked, but Churchill, like many Londoners, showed the 'Blitz Spirit' and did not leave.

The cat did once hide in a drawer during an air raid, though, prompting Churchill to quip, according to Brendon's source, 'Shame on you, bearing a name such as yours, to skulk there while the enemy is overhead.' As Britain's outlook worsened and Nazi bombs fell more heavily on London, the decision was made to evacuate Nelson to Chequers, the country home of the British Prime Minister.

Smoky, a fluffy dark Persian, replaced him as the Downing Street cat. Smoky had been living in the Cabinet Office next door and was seemingly less fazed by the chaos of war. Smoky was allowed into Churchill's quarters and slept on the bed, just as Nelson had done.

Following a serious Cabinet leak, the head of MI6, Sir Stewart Menzies, visited Churchill in the prime ministerial bedroom. During their conversation, Smoky moved onto the windowsill, causing Churchill to quip, 'You see it is as I thought – my cat is signalling with his tail to the pelicans in the park.'

As well as his older cats, Churchill had, like many people, a particularly soft spot for kittens. Richard Langworth, in his book *Churchill by Himself: In His Own Words*, recounts how Churchill was once offered a litter brought in a basket by a neighbour to Chartwell. He had already been warned by housekeepers and other staff that there was no room for any more animals on the estate; however, the sight of these beautiful white kittens wearing red bows was too much for Winston to resist. They had only been in his bedroom for an hour, investigating their surroundings and clawing and tearing into everything in sight, when he realised that Chartwell had just gained a whole gang of cats to care for indefinitely. 'Take these kittens away before I fall in love,' he ordered dejectedly. Churchill knew he could not take just one of the kittens – a dilemma so many of us would have faced.

Both Churchill and his wife, Clementine, were known to refer to one another with animal names: she was 'Cat' and he was 'Pug'. He and Clementine woofed and miaowed at each other in private (perhaps the less you question that, the more it makes sense), and they referred to their children as 'the kittens'. For Churchill, it seems, an animal was really not so far off being a person – if not human then at least comparable in terms of commanding respect and affection.

In October 1953, Churchill was midway through his post-war premiership, but he had been incapacitated by a stroke suffered earlier in the year. Despite being under a physician's care, he gave a speech to the Conservative Party conference in Margate on 10 October. Back at Downing Street, he was in a good mood as he listened to the news coverage of it on the wireless as he felt it had gone well, when a small black kitten suddenly jumped up on his knee. The cat had recently been found on the step of No. 10 and brought into the house. It turned out to be a very lucky moment for the animal. 'It has brought me luck,' he said, stroking the happy cat. 'It shall be called Margate.'

Churchill often thought of animals during the war, particularly in times of mass casualties. As he reflected on the mass bombing of Germany, he was reportedly in tears: 'Tens of thousands of lives were extinguished in one night. Old men, old women, little children, yes, yes, children about to be born and, and pussy cats.'

Churchill was also very moved by the bombing of Hiroshima and Nagasaki. His research assistant Denis Kelly wrote that Churchill declared, 'The worst thing Truman and I did was to throw that bloody bomb. And think of all the poor little dogs and pussy-cats.' Kelly recalled that 'it was said with such passionate sincerity that none of us even smiled'.

As well as domestic cats, Churchill loved big cats too. One of his favourites was a young female leopard named Sheba, presented to him in 1953 by Nuri al-Said, a pro-British Iraqi politician. Press reports claimed, perhaps dubiously, that his secretary Anthony Montague Browne unboxed the 21-month-old Sheba on the Cabinet table, while Churchill petted and fed the animal in her crate. Montague Browne stated that Sheba was 'an adorable fifteen-pound ball of fluff'. When Sheba grew too ferocious, she was moved to London Zoo and Churchill visited her and Rota and petted them through the bars.

Originally named Rotaprince, the lion was born in a circus

in 1938. A Mr George Thomson later won him in a bet and kept him in his back garden in north-west London.

Having outgrown his cage, Rota was given to Churchill by Thomson in appreciation for the north African victories in the Second World War. Churchill kept him for a time, but later Rota joined a number of Churchill's other animals at London Zoo. Rota was a popular lion, featuring in newsreels and as an animal closely associated with the wartime leader. Thomson was a keen publicist too, arguing Rota should have taken part in the Second World War victory parade.

Sadly, Rota had to be put down in 1955. Churchill was upset upon receiving a telegram from Thomson saying: 'POOR OLD ROTA GOD BLESS HIM DEAR OLD CHAP.'

Churchill wanted Rota to have a decent burial, but Thomson sensed yet another commercial opportunity and, much to Churchill's disgust, opted to stuff poor Rota in a roaring posture and put him on display in a Piccadilly showroom. Brendon notes, however, that Churchill did manage to veto the use of a plaque reading 'I'd provide the roar'. Rota was bought by an American in 1956 and moved to the Lightner Museum in St Augustine, Florida, where he resides to this day, now behind glass.

Dogs were as much a part of Churchill's life as cats, horses and the rest of his menagerie. In *My Dear Mr Churchill* by Walter Graebner, Churchill is quoted as saying, 'No one should not know the companionship of a dog. There is nothing like it.' Churchill's most famous dogs were two miniature poodles: Rufus and his successor, Rufus II. The first Rufus rarely left Churchill's side during the war, even accompanying him into the Cabinet Room while ministers were discussing serious matters of war. 'No, Rufus, I haven't found it necessary to ask you to join the wartime Cabinet,' Churchill was recorded as saying at one point.

Tragically, Rufus was knocked down and killed by a car in October 1947. As with Tango the cat, the sad news of his beloved dog's demise was initially kept from Churchill as he was attending the Conservative Party conference at the time. When he was informed, Churchill was extremely upset and started to look for a substitute. He was assisted in this task by Graebner, the American journalist who arranged for *Life* magazine to serialise Churchill's war memoirs. Another poodle was supplied, this one called Rufus II in tribute to his fallen predecessor. Churchill grew just as attached to Rufus II despite him having a more difficult temperament.

Rufus ate with his master, sat on his lap and had his own special chair. The dog was also the first to be served at dinner by the butler, which he ate in the dining room on a cloth on the ground next to Churchill. Churchill enjoyed films and one night, while he and his family were gathered watching *Oliver Twist*, Churchill hurriedly covered the dog's eyes at the scene of Bill Sykes drowning his dog, Bullseye. 'Don't look now dear. I'll tell you about it afterwards,' he gently warned Rufus II.

Rufus II was also called upon to help bring some pups into the world. In January 1955, he received a proposal from 'Jennifer', described as a 'standard poodle, first-class pedigree, very accomplished and a nice good-tempered character'. Rufus was asked to consider 'giving me your kind services so that I can have some puppies by you'. A telegram was sent in reply: 'I AM CONSIDERING YOUR PROPOSAL AND WILL COMMUNICATE WITH YOU SHORTLY. RUFUS.'

Churchill was delighted at the prospect, despite opposition from his aides, so Jennifer was informed:

> My dear Jennifer,
>
> On the 10th of April I shall be going to stay with a great friend of mine, Miss Lobban, who has very nice kennels in London. I should be very glad to receive you there; and Miss Lobban says she will make every arrangement for your comfort.

This letter was marked 'VERY PRIVATE'.

Brendon notes that when Rufus II died in 1962, Churchill was saddened by the death of his companion of many years, 'whose intimacy had assuaged not only the cares of senescence but the loneliness of leadership. He was my closest confidant.' Rufus and Rufus II were buried next to each other at Chartwell, with Jock the cat later laid to rest alongside them.

Another pet much beloved by Churchill was Toby the budgerigar, one of many that he owned over the years. Legend has it that before the war Churchill owned a beautiful yellow and blue macaw named Charlie who screeched obscenities about Hitler, but this is just an urban myth. Presented as a gift in 1954, Toby had a beautiful golden face and blue-green colouring. According to Brendon, the bird 'strutted across the dining table, knocked over glasses, helped himself to grapefruit, fought with his reflection in the silver pepper pot and chattered like a schoolgirl at a picnic'. Toby even tried whisky and 'apparently once fell into his master's brandy glass'. Toby also lapped ink from his master's pen, 'embellishing his letters with blots and scribbles ... He nibbled the edges of book and proof pages' – an indication, in Churchill's view, that Toby had read them: 'Oh! Yes, that's all right, give him the next chapter!' Tragically Toby disappeared in 1961 when Churchill was staying at the Hôtel de Paris in Monte Carlo. Toby was spooked by something and in a panic flew out of the window. A large reward was offered, but he was never seen again. Churchill was heartbroken.

Solace perhaps came in the shape of the many other animals Churchill had access to, some of which were diplomatic gifts. Live animals have long been exchanged by world leaders as a mechanism for strengthening ties between nations, although the practice is much rarer today. China in particular is known for its 'panda diplomacy'. Unsurprisingly, when London Zoo received its first giant pandas at the end of 1938, Churchill rushed to see them, especially a cub called Ming – 'Brightness' in Mandarin. Brendon describes how 'Ming inspired panda mania: there were panda books, panda hats, panda toys, panda jokes, panda charms, panda wallpapers, panda cigarette cases.' *The Times* observed that 'one of the country's more benevolent elder politicians has been discreetly compared with a panda', almost certainly referencing Churchill himself.

As well as 'panda diplomacy', there was 'platypus diplomacy'. In 1943, Churchill telegrammed John Curtin, the Australian Prime Minister, requesting six platypuses be immediately sent to Britain. David Fleay, an eminent Australian biologist, declared that transporting the animals halfway across the world in the middle of a world war was not a feasible plan. Fleay suggested that, if it must be done, a single platypus could be sent. He named it Winston and sent him on his way. Sadly, the platypus died at sea during a highly turbulent voyage, rather proving Fleay's point. Various historians have sought to put this bizarre episode into some sort of context, but it seems as though Churchill simply wanted a platypus. More seriously, the Australians wanted good relations with the UK and Churchill at this time as they also needed weapons and equipment such as Spitfire planes. There were various disagreements about how the war had been fought and in regard to the allocation of munitions to Australia, so this form of animal diplomacy did serve a clear purpose.

Churchill did not like all animals though. He viewed rabbits as cowardly and weak and often used them as the basis of derogatory comparisons: fleeing enemy soldiers and politicians such as R. A. Butler were described as behaving like scared rabbits. As Kay Halle notes in *The Irrepressible Churchill*, 'When asked whether Neville Chamberlain's attempt to intimidate Attlee over appeasement was not like a snake dominating a rabbit, Churchill replied, "It's more like a rabbit dominating a lettuce." Even in the early days of Nazism, Churchill was critical of Hitler and used animal imagery to hammer home his point. He spoke of the 'fable of the jackal who went hunting with the tiger and what happened after the hunt was over'. Fascist Italy was not spared such comparisons, with Mussolini described as a jackal and a hyena, while Bolshevik Russia was variously characterised as a collection of snakes, vultures, crocodiles, wolves, bears and hyenas, Brendon notes.

Vultures were another key feature of his speeches, which is perhaps unsurprising at a time when air power was more relevant to warfare than humans had ever known before. In the interwar years, he warned of the vultures of protectionism and socialism at home. He later called those bombarding Britain 'vultures' and called for their 'nests' on the mainland to be attacked in turn. Brendon quotes Churchill as saying, 'Two vultures hung over Britain in 1941. The threat of invasion and the assault of the Luftwaffe.' Other vultures of uncertainty poised above him, Churchill said: his anxieties about the D-Day invasion, his concerns about the continuing war with Japan and his apprehensions about the outcome of the 1945 general election. Soon after the Labour Party's victory at the polls, he commiserated with Conservative supporters by declaring Labour the 'gloomy vultures of nationalisation'.

Churchill had encountered hippos on a trip to Egypt and found them a very dangerous animal. He could be wary of more exotic animals, Brendon explains, although he used also the imagery of animal to political effect in speeches to convey stoicism, stability and strength. On 9 May 1945 Churchill praised London's people as 'like a great rhinoceros, a great hippopotamus' in facing down the Nazis.

In his younger years, Churchill had witnessed William Ewart Gladstone giving his last speech at the House of Commons dispatch box on 1 March 1894. He later described the former Prime

Minister as 'like a great white eagle, at once fierce and splendid'. Of course, Churchill mostly associated the eagle with America, given the bald eagle is the national bird of the United States.

On his eightieth birthday in 1954, Churchill was immortalised in a special coin minted for the occasion. Parliamentarians gathered in Westminster Hall to pay tribute to his service and especially his wartime leadership. In response to this praise, he stated, 'It was a nation and race dwelling all around the globe that had the lion's heart. I had the luck to be called upon to give the roar. I also hope that I sometimes suggested to the lion the right place to use his claws.'

Throughout his life, Churchill became increasingly supportive of animal welfare and was horrified at any mistreatment, such as the starving dogs he had seen in the Mediterranean during the First World War. He was unable to leave any animal near to him in pain or suffering. When his valet's dog injured its paw, he paid for it to stay in a dog's hospital for a fortnight because, he said, 'I can't bear to see it limping around.' Richard Langworth writes of Churchill that 'an enormously agreeable side of his character was his attitude toward animals', while Sir Anthony Montague Browne, his last private secretary, said of him, 'Although a Victorian – and they were not notably aware of animal suffering – he had a sensitivity well in advance of his time.'

Even in childhood, Churchill's grandmother described him as a bulldog; the Second World War crystallised the image. Sir Alexander Cadogan, head of the Foreign Office, called Churchill 'theatrically bulldogish' during the evacuation of Dunkirk. Churchill arguably even resembled a bulldog, with the jowls, the jaw and the square frame. Many items and artefacts – from figurines and souvenirs to cartoons, posters and miscellaneous memorabilia – were all modelled in this bulldog image.

A great lover of animals throughout his life, political and private, perhaps Churchill himself was the original, and most enduring, political animal.

CHAPTER THREE

A HISTORY OF PRESIDENTIAL PETS

'Any man who does not like dogs ... does not deserve to be in the White House.'
CALVIN COOLIDGE, PRESIDENT OF
THE UNITED STATES 1923–29

Of the forty-five men who have been President of the United States, only two have not livened up the corridors and residence of the White House with the happy thump of paws and burst of energy that a pet brings: Donald Trump and James K. Polk (1845–49). To compile even a comprehensive list of all the presidential pets would require an entire book (and good ones have already been written on this topic), but some of the fascinating highlights I have outlined below.

George Washington held office from 1789 to 1797, although the White House had not even been built when he was elected. He was a keen foxhunter, then a far more widely accepted pastime than it is today. In addition to the many horses in his stables, Washington also kept at least forty hounds, whose names included Madam Moose, Sweet Lips, True Love, Taster, Forester, Tipler and Vulcan. The First Lady, Martha Washington, had a green parrot. The couples' favourite granddaughter, Nelly Parke Custis, adored the bird.

Washington's successor, John Adams (1797–1801), was also a keen horseman. He built the first presidential stables, which were home to his favourite horse, Cleopatra.

The third President, Thomas Jefferson (1801–09), was a keen proponent of animal rights; however, as a slave owner, human rights appeared less of a priority for Jefferson, as well as many of his contemporaries. He adored animals, allowing partridges, pheasants and peacocks to roam the forests of his Monticello estate in Virginia. As Niall Kelly notes in *Presidential Pets*, Jefferson sent Captain Meriwether Lewis to explore the 'wild' west in 1804. Lewis is best known for leading the exploration of the territory gained through the Louisiana Purchase. On returning from his travels, Lewis gave the President several grizzly bears, who were allowed to walk around on a leash on the White House lawn. Jefferson's political opponents, the Federalists, scorned this use of the White House grounds, nicknaming them 'the President's Bear Garden'. Jefferson also kept several mockingbirds. His favourite, Dick, was allowed to fly freely around the Oval Office and sometimes sang the President to sleep. Dick also learned how to 'accompany' Jefferson as he played the violin.

James Monroe, President from 1817 to 1825, owned two sheepdogs, a gift from the Marquis de Lafayette. Monroe's daughter, Hester Maria, also had a black spaniel she loved dearly.

During the American Civil War, in which over 600,000 people lost their lives, animals began to take on a much more significant role as emblems of the nation. Some Civil War soldiers adopted animals as mascots. One of these was Jack, a dog who originally belonged to a Confederate jailer until the canine decided he preferred the company of Union prisoners. Jack accompanied them to a prisoner of war camp in Salisbury, North Carolina, and he was later released as part of a prisoner exchange, eventually finding himself at Fortress Monroe. Mascots like Jack not only provided physical help such as locating food and water sources but were also a great comfort to soldiers, being a reliable friend in very trying times. Stonewall the dog became the mascot for a group of artillerymen, the Richmond Howitzers, and even joined the line of soldiers for roll call. They valued him so highly that he was carried around battles in a chest in case he was lost or killed while battlefield positions changed.

Another stalwart of Civil War mascots was the eagle. Andrew Hager, who has been historian in residence at the Presidential Pet Museum since 2017, notes that a regiment of volunteers from Wisconsin travelled with a bald eagle called Old Abe, who took part in battles, flying and screeching above the rebel army. The eagle was targeted by sharpshooters, Hager writes, but survived the war and lived out his life in the Wisconsin State Capitol.

John Quincy Adams (1825–29) may or may not have had an alligator in the White House. The story goes that in 1826 the Marquis de Lafayette came to stay in the White House for two months, bringing the reptile with him. The alligator apparently lived in a bathtub and left with Lafayette. According to Hager, this is an apocryphal tale, but it is true that Emperor Ninkō of Japan sent seven small dogs to Quincy Adams. The breed was Japanese Chin, commonly called 'sleeve dogs' because they fit inside the sleeve of a kimono. They were sent as a sign of thanks that the United States had opened relations with the isolated kingdom. The significance of the breed and the number of dogs given are a clear display of the importance of animal diplomacy even at this relatively early stage in US history. Less dramatically, Quincy Adams and his wife Louisa were also known to rear silkworms.

Poll the parrot was a particularly quirky presidential pet. Poll belonged to Andrew Jackson, President from 1829–37, and is most famous for reportedly having been removed from the President's funeral for saying rude things during the service, although historians dispute this. Poll, nicknamed Polly, was looked after by Jackson's nephew William Donelson, who described the bird as 'fat and saucy' in one letter – something the funeral attendees apparently discovered on 10 June 1845. The Reverend William Menefee, quoted in *Andrew Jackson and Early Tennessee History* by Samuel Gordon Heiskell and John Sevier, said Poll 'got excited and commenced swearing so *loud* and *long* as to disturb the people and had to be carried from the house'.

William Henry Harrison was President only for a month before he died. Harrison wanted to present himself to voters as an outdoorsman and lover of nature to cement his image as a man of the people in touch with the land and its animals, in a clear case of animals being employed for political purposes. Part of this included giving the impression to the public that he had been a farmer, despite having grown up in luxury in a mansion in the state of Virginia. When he moved into 1600 Pennsylvania Avenue, he brought with him a cow called Sukey.

John Tyler (1841–45) succeeded Harrison. A widower on taking office, in 1843 he celebrated his engagement to Julia Gardiner by presenting her with two wolfhounds. His favourite pets were a canary called John Ty and a horse named The General. As Kelly notes, when the horse died, he was buried in sight of the President's window under the South Lawn at Sherwood Forest,

Tyler's home in Virginia. The epitaph reads: 'Here lies the body of my good horse, The General. For years he bore me around the circuit of my practice and all that time he never made a blunder. Would that his master could say the same.'

Zachary Taylor, President from 1849 to 1850, was a military man and, unsurprisingly, he was particularly fond of horses. His favourite steed was Old Whitey, though the animal was actually more of a shade of grey. Old Whitey came with Taylor to Washington and grazed on the White House lawn. So devoted was the animal that he even stood behind the coffin of his master when Taylor died only sixteen months into office.

Taylor's successor, Millard Fillmore (1850–53), founded the American Society for the Prevention of Cruelty to Animals. Like Jefferson before him, human suffering was evidently less of a priority in his eyes, as he was firmly pro-slavery.

James Buchanan held office from 1857 to 1861. He was the only President who never married, and he was an animal lover too. He once received a pair of bald eagles from a friend in San Francisco. During the day, the birds roamed freely around Wheatland, his Pennsylvania estate, and they were caged outside at night. Kelly quotes a visitor to Wheatland who once wrote, 'These birds of love, as if conscious that they nestled beneath the eye of the Chief Magistrate of this great Republic, seem to plume themselves on their associations… and although apparently as free as when at home on the Sierra Nevada, show no disposition to wing their flight from Wheatland.' Buchanan was also once presented with two elephants from the King of Siam (now known as Thailand), but the animals apparently never made it to the United States.

Kelly writes that, just as Abraham Lincoln's life was marred by tragedy, so too was that of his childhood pig. When the animal became bacon for the family, he was so upset that for the rest of his life he was compassionate towards animals. As a father, he allowed his sons as many pets as they wanted. Lincoln was President between 1861 and 1865, and two years into his presidency he was presented with a live turkey as a gift for their dinner table. However, his son Tad adored the bird and wanted to keep it. The boy got his way and the turkey, which they named Jack, survived and became yet another beloved White House pet. In 1864, a booth was erected on White House grounds so that soldiers stationed there could vote. Lincoln noticed Jack walking amongst the crowds and asked his son whether the turkey had voted. Tad replied, 'He's not of age yet.'

One of Lincoln's favourite dogs, Fido, became a national symbol of grief after the President's assassination. *Cartes-de-visite* (calling cards) were popular at the time, and a photograph of Fido became strongly associated with the assassinated President. Sadly, Fido was also killed. He had lived with family friends of the Lincolns following the President's death, but he was later stabbed by a drunk and his body was found in a graveyard in Springfield, Illinois, where he had taken shelter.

Lincoln's successor was Andrew Johnson (1865–69), a farmer who took some of his New Jersey cows to Washington upon becoming President. He was kind to even the smallest animals. On one occasion he found a family of mice in his bedroom, but instead of killing them, he served them flour and water.

Ulysses S. Grant (1869–77) was an equestrian President. Legend has it that Grant raced his horses through the streets of Washington and was once fined by a policeman who did not recognise him. Grant also had many dogs, including one named Cincinnatus, a gift from the citizens of Cincinnati. Grant's youngest son Jesse was also very fond of dogs, but they all met tragic and mysterious ends. Nowadays, White House staff usually dote on presidential pets, but when Jesse was given another pup, a Newfoundland named Faithful, President Grant warned his staff, 'Jesse has a new dog. You may have noticed that his former pets have been peculiarly unfortunate. When this dog dies every employee in the White House will be at once discharged.' Faithful and her successors lived long, happy lives after this stern warning.

'Noah's Collection' was the nickname given to the next President's menagerie. Rutherford B. Hayes, who served for one term from 1877 to 1881, and his First Lady Lucy kept many animals at the White House. Though they didn't come in pairs, there were probably enough of them to fill an ark. Lucy Hayes's love of animals became renowned worldwide, prompting the US Consul in Siam to send her a Siamese kitten, the first of its breed to grace the US. As Kelly notes, the Consul, David Sickels, wrote:

Dear Madam,

Having observed a few months ago in an American newspaper a statement that you were fond of cats, I have taken the liberty of forwarding to you one of the finest specimens of Siamese cats that I have been able to procure in this country. Miss Pussy goes to Hong Kong whence she will be transhipped by the Occidental and Oriental line, in charge of the Purser, to San Francisco and then sent by express to Washington. I am informed that this is the first attempt ever made to send a Siamese cat to America.

The Hayes family promptly changed Miss Pussy's name to Siam, and they grew extremely fond of her, though sadly she was struck down by a sudden illness within a year and perished. Hayes was also fond of his dogs, including his greyhound, Grim, of whom he wrote, 'He is good-natured and neat in his habits, and took all our hearts at once.'

Animal welfare standards were changing at this time, with Hayes the first President to bring such matters to greater attention on the national stage: in the 1878 State of the Union speech he discussed his desire that animals in transit should be treated better; many died as they were being transported across the United States, as Hager notes.

James Garfield was President for less than seven months in 1881 before he was assassinated. His dog, a Newfoundland, was called Veto, a name said to be intended as a reminder to Congress that Garfield might not pass every bill they proposed. A highly intelligent dog, Veto helped avert disaster by barking to alert White House staff to a fire in a barn. On another occasion, a horse became spooked and as the animal panicked, Veto got hold of its reins with his mouth and had at least some control of the animal before stable staff could calm it down.

Garfield was a big fan of Charles Dickens, and the author gave readings at the White House when on tours of the United States. As Kelly notes, during *A Christmas Carol*, Dickens delivered the words, 'Bless his heart: it's Fezziwig again!' and a dog started barking. This left Dickens laughing so much he could barely continue his story. When Garfield came across those who had attended the reading, he greeted them by saying: 'Bow! Wow! Wow!'

Grover Cleveland (1885–89 and 1893–97) and his wife Frances – who had once been his ward – owned various animals. These included a Japanese poodle, canaries and a mockingbird. In 1893, the US Consul in Bremen, Germany, sent Frances Cleveland three dachshunds, at that stage rare animals in the US.

Benjamin Harrison (1889–93) had a pet goat named Old Whiskers who pulled his grandchildren around the White House grounds in a cart, although he sometimes escaped and had to be brought back to the fold. Harrison also presented his grandchildren with a dog named Dash, as well as two possums, Mr Reciprocity and Mr Protection, named after two political foundations of Republican thought at the time.

The most beloved pet of William McKinley (1897–1901) was a double-yellow-headed Amazon parrot named Washington Post, who was a present from a friend and worth thousands of dollars. The bird was known to chat away to White House visitors; his cage was deliberately positioned so that he could see everyone's comings and goings. He allegedly croaked, 'Oh, look at all the pretty girls' as women walked by. McKinley claimed Washington Post was the most intelligent bird he had ever met and that he was capable of finishing the President's tunes when he hummed such favourites as 'Yankee Doodle Dandy'.

Not all Presidents of this era had household pets, but they did all have horses. Until the early twentieth century, horses were the main means of transport. They became both victims and winners as industrialisation rapidly advanced. Their numbers declined as they were used less for work, but they did start to become viewed more as family pets and useful for leisure.

The first new President of the twentieth century, Theodore Roosevelt (1901–09) had around forty pets, winning the prize for the President who had the largest number of animals at the White House. Amongst their number were five guinea pigs (Admiral Dewey, Dr Johnson, Bishop Doane, Fighting Bob Evans and Father O'Grady); Maude the pig; Josiah the badger, a gift from a little girl in Kansas when Roosevelt toured her state by train during his 1903 presidential campaign; Eli Yale the blue macaw; a rabbit called Peter; a barn owl; a hyena named Bill, who was a gift from the Emperor of Ethiopia; and a one-legged rooster. Let's not forget the Roosevelts' dogs: Sailor Boy, the Chesapeake retriever; a mongrel named Skip; their black, smooth-haired Manchester terrier Blackjack, known as Jack for short; and Manchu, a black Pekinese, who was a gift to his daughter Alice from the last Empress of China. Alice also had a snake which she would wear round her neck to shock guests. She named it Emily Spinach because it was 'green as spinach and as thin as my Aunt Emily'.

Roosevelt and his six children clearly loved animals. In a letter to Mrs Roswell Field on 27 July 1901, Roosevelt wrote, 'It is a real pleasure to send you a photograph of my boy Kermit, with Jack, the Manchester terrier, who is absolutely a member of the family.' However, Blackjack was less popular with Tom Quartz, the Roosevelt family cat who terrorised the dog at every turn, although he was known to be extremely fierce and 'playful' with humans too, once chasing the Speaker of the House of Representatives,

Joseph G. Cannon, down the White House stairs. But despite Blackjack's fear of Tom Quartz, Roosevelt rated the dog's prowess: 'Jack was human in his intelligence and affection; he learned all kinds of tricks, was a high-bred gentleman, never brawled, and was a dauntless fighter.'

Blackjack was initially buried behind the White House but was later exhumed because First Lady Edith Roosevelt said she did not want him 'beneath the eyes of Presidents who might care nothing for little black dogs'. In 1908, at the end of Roosevelt's second term of office, Blackjack's coffin was again exhumed and reburied at the Roosevelts' Long Island estate, Sagamore Hill. In 1999, another breed of terrier was named after the twenty-sixth President: the Teddy Roosevelt terrier.

Another Roosevelt cat was the six-toed Slippers, who once famously lay across the carpet and refused to budge while a line of visiting ambassadors was being led through to the dining room. The President insisted that the dignitaries not disturb Slippers and instead walk around him. Seemingly, in the White House under Roosevelt cats were also considered VIPs.

Of the forty or so pets, most belonged to his children, but as an animal lover Roosevelt was pleased to have the beasts around. Some of the family's animals were not particularly suitable for the White House, with macaws, zebras, raccoons, roosters, pigs and rats sent at various stages to the family's Long Island summer house. But Algonquin the pony stayed. A five-year-old Quentin Roosevelt apparently once brought Algonquin up the White House elevator to visit his brother Charlie while he was sick and stuck in bed. Like his sister Alice, Quentin also enjoyed pranking guests and was known to roller-skate around the White House with snakes wrapped around his arms. He was quite the wild child.

William Howard Taft (1909–13) and his First Lady, Nellie Taft, felt so strongly about cows that they kept one on the White House lawn to provide them with high-quality milk daily. Mooly Wooly was their first cow, who was succeeded by another named Pauline Wayne.

Hager notes that when the opera singer Enrico Caruso performed for the Tafts, he presented their daughter Helen with a small white dog, which she named Caruso in his honour. Caruso was a very famous singer at the time and knew that his legacy in the White House would be secured through the gift of the animal.

Woodrow Wilson (1913–21), an intellectual, did not come from an agricultural background and so was not as attached to country pursuits as some of his predecessors. However, he did keep sheep on the White House lawn. During the First World War, he brought a ram named Old Ike to Washington so that Ike and his flock could keep the lawn tidy while the gardeners were shipped to the trenches of France. As a bonus, they also provided wool for clothing. Ike was seldom seen without tobacco in his mouth, chewing away. After his job at the White House was done, Kelly notes that Old Ike was given to a Mr Probert from the Associated Press and lived out his long retirement as a nicotine addict; he was even given a last wad to chew on when he was put down due to old age in 1927.

Wilson's health never improved after he suffered a stroke in 1919. In the last two years of his presidency, he was given a specially trained bull terrier named Bruce as a 'therapy dog', a first for the time.

The popularity of Rin Tin Tin, a German shepherd and the first doggy movie star, was such that the breed became a regular at the White House, for instance owned by Herbert Hoover, Hager notes. More recently, Joe Biden had them at the White House too (see next chapter).

But it was the twenty-ninth President, Warren Harding (1921–23), who had the first proper celebrity White House dog. Harding initially made friends with a squirrel named Pete when he moved into the White House, and guests often brought the rodent nuts. But it was Harding's favourite pooch, an Airedale called Laddie Boy, who became most associated with the President. The dog was born on 26 July 1920 in Toledo, Ohio, and arrived on 5 March 1921 to the White House. The Hardings held a birthday party for Laddie Boy each year for which they would invite the neighbourhood dogs to enjoy a cake made of multiple layers of dog biscuits. The dog even had his own seat at meetings the President attended and took part in activities as diverse as leading the White House Easter Egg Roll, attending all manner of glitzy presidential functions, leading the Humane Society's 'Be Kind to Animals' parade and 'writing' letters to newspapers (of which Harding himself, of course, was the author). As a newspaperman before entering politics, Harding had devoted some articles to animal welfare. In one, in the *Marion Daily Star*, an Ohio paper, Harding wrote that 'whether the Creator planned it so, or environment and human companionship have made it so, men may learn richly from the love and fidelity of a brave and devoted dog'.

In 1922, the *New York Times* published one of Laddie Boy's many letters:

> So many people express a wish to see me, and I shake hands with so many callers at the Executive Mansion, that I fear there are some people who will suspect me of political inclinations. From what I see of politics, I am sure I have no such aspirations.

Laddie Boy the media darling 'planted the idea of White House pets firmly in the popular imagination', according to Hager. Toy companies tried to persuade Harding to give them exclusive rights to sell soft toys in Laddie Boy's image, but Harding refused to endorse any particular stuffed animal. Hager observed that 'given the deep-seated corruption of many officials in his administration, this principled stance feels highly ironic'.

Harding died in 1923. In *Presidential Pets*, Kelly quotes the Associated Press report on the day of his passing:

> There was one member of the White House household today who couldn't quite comprehend the air of sadness which overhung the executive mansion. It was Laddie Boy, President Harding's Airedale friend and companion. Coming to the White House a raw-boned, callow pup, Laddie Boy has, in two years, grown to the estate of dignity and wholesome respect for his official surroundings.

Laddie Boy was perhaps one of the most popular presidential pets of all time. When he died in 1929, newsboys from across the country sent one penny each to the White House to honour the fact Harding had once been part of the newspaper industry. The coins, nearly 20,000 of them, were then melted down and formed into a statue by the sculptor Bashka Paeff. It was intended as a gift for Mrs Harding, but she died before it could be presented to her, so it was donated to the Smithsonian Museum, where it still stands.

Calvin Coolidge (1923–29) received a number of pets as gifts, but these animals often ended up being donated to zoos as it was not possible to keep them on site at the White House. These included a pygmy hippo from South Africa, a bear from Mexico, a wallaby from Australia, a goose called Enoch, a donkey named Ebenezer, two lion cubs, a bobcat and an antelope.

Blackie, one of the three Coolidge (house)cats, with a name perhaps more reflective of that time than now, was known to adore riding up and down in the plush White House elevator. When another of their cats, Tiger, disappeared, Coolidge used the new radio technology to broadcast an appeal for his missing cat, who was duly returned. The President and his wife, Grace, had a number of improbably named dogs, including Tiny Tim (who became Terrible Tim), Blackberry, Ruby Rough and Palo Alto. His favourite, though, was Oshkosh, a white collie also known as Rob Roy. Journalists were expressly warned not to step on the toes of the beloved pet. Prudence Prim was the First Lady's favourite collie, and she was known to dress up the animal in floppy hats with ribbon trimmings for events such as her garden parties, as Kelly notes. The Coolidges treated their dogs so well that a guest declared:

> They was feeding the dogs so much that at one time it looked

to me like the dogs was getting more than I was. The butler was so slow in bringing one course that I come pretty near getting down on my all fours and barking to see if business wouldn't pick up with me!

Rob Roy slept in the President's bedroom and had his own portrait painted alongside the First Lady, which can be seen in the White House to this day. It was said that the collie had to be bribed with treats to keep still while sitting for the painting.

Grace Coolidge also owned a beloved raccoon named Rebecca. The President would take her for evening walks on a leash around the White House lawns. It's said that Rebecca was partial to taking a bath, mainly because she enjoyed playing with the soap.

The Coolidges clearly felt the deaths of their animals as keenly as any true pet lover does. Prudence Prim died in South Dakota in 1927 with the family while they were on their summer holiday. Coolidge wrote in his autobiography, 'We lost her in the Black Hills. She lies out there in the shadow of Bear Butte where the Indians told me the Great Spirit came to commune with his children.' In 1928, Rob Roy fell ill and died despite Coolidge's best efforts, going as far as attempting to get him treated at the Walter Reed Army Hospital, notes Hager. In a tribute to Rob Roy, Coolidge wrote in his autobiography, 'His especial delight was to ride with me in the boats when I went fishing. So although I know he would bark for joy as the grim boatman ferried him across the dark waters of the Styx, yet his going left me lonely on the hither shore.'

Herbert Hoover (1929–33) is a prime example of a politician making full use of the electoral advantage brought by being perceived as an animal lover. He owned King Tut, a Belgian Malinois breed, which is a variety of the Belgian shepherd dog. A friend had presented Hoover with the pooch when it was about a year old and Tut soon became a beloved family member. Hoover was advised that he came across as too cold, so it was decided that King Tut should join him in campaign photographs to help present him in a warmer light. Print journalism was in its heyday and photographs of politicians were a key way in which they came across to the electorate, far more so than in our age of digital video. It is thought by some, both then and now, that without King Tut to soften his image, Hoover would have lost the election. Apparently, while Hoover read the newspapers on the White House lawn, King Tut would sit on the pages already read and discarded on the lawn – a sort of doggy paperweight.

Franklin Delano Roosevelt, who was President from 1933 to 1945, received Fala the black Scottish terrier as a present. Fala's bed was situated at the end of Roosevelt's own. The dog was well treated and had a bone every morning for breakfast, which was brought up on a tray alongside the President's breakfast. Fala perhaps overindulged and so was at one point put on a diet (although he certainly wasn't the only political animal to put on a little weight, as we will discover in later chapters).

In 1944, during the Second World War, a rumour spread that Fala, who accompanied FDR everywhere, had been left behind on a remote island in the Pacific Ocean. Roosevelt's Republican rivals back in Washington claimed that a Navy ship had been sent to retrieve Fala at a cost of millions of dollars to the US taxpayer, but this was a fabrication. In one of his fireside chats to the nation, Roosevelt raged:

The Republican leaders have not been content with attacks on me, my wife or my sons. No, not content with that, they now include my little dog, Fala. Well of course I don't resent such attacks, my family doesn't resent attacks, but Fala does. You know Fala is Scotch and being a Scottie, as soon as he learned that the Republican fiction writers in Congress had concocted a story that I had left him behind on the Aleutian Islands and had sent a destroyer back to find him at a cost to the taxpayers of two or three, or eight or twenty million dollars – his Scotch soul was furious. He has not been the same dog since.

'The Fala speech', which was given to the International Brotherhood of Teamsters labour union and carried on the radio across the United States, became very politically important in the 1944 presidential election and was thought by many to be very funny. The union members were so entertained that one hammered a silver tray with a ladle, with another grabbing wine bottles and smashing glasses in their glee.

Fala spent less than five years at the White House. During that time, Hager notes, Fala appeared in two Metro-Goldwyn-Mayer newsreels. One, broadcast in 1943, was called simply *Fala: The President's Dog*, in which FDR made Fala earn treats by performing tricks. The narrator, pretending to be the President, says, 'The more I hear of the Nazis, the more I love my dog.' Fala also met world leaders and had a cameo in an Oscar-winning comedy, *Princess O'Rourke*. He became even more popular after FDR was re-elected in 1944 and even had his own secretary to help with his fan mail… of which he received more than his master.

During the Battle of the Bulge, December 1944 to January

1945, Fala even became a counter-espionage asset. The pooch was so well-known that any unfamiliar soldiers arriving in US positions were asked for the name of the President's dog as an extra level of security against saboteurs.

His fame aside, Fala was a beloved pet, and his huge importance to FDR is made clear in that the dog is buried less than ten yards away from FDR's own grave. First Lady Eleanor Roosevelt said that although Fala had accepted her after her husband's death, she 'was just someone to put up with until the master should return'. Fala is immortalised by Roosevelt's side at his presidential memorial in Washington DC – the only White House pet to have this honour.

PART II

THE POLITICAL ANIMALS OF THE WHITE HOUSE

CHAPTER FOUR

POST-WAR PRESIDENTIAL PETS

'You want a friend in Washington? Get a dog.'
HARRY TRUMAN, PRESIDENT OF
THE UNITED STATES 1945–53

Despite being responsible for perhaps the best-known of all quotations about politics and animals, the thirty-third President had no great love for pets. This cost Truman early on in his presidency, when he decided he did not, in fact, want to keep his cocker spaniel puppy, Feller, and instead gave it to the White House physician. Feller's change of ownership made headline news and it went down like a lead balloon with America's animal-loving electorate.

Later, Truman's First Lady, Bess, was given an Irish setter, Mike, by Postmaster General Bob Hannigan. Alas, some of the White House policemen were too generous with their treats, so an overweight Mike was sent to live at a farmhouse in Virginia. Although President Truman was not an animal lover, his daughter Margaret certainly was; she even wrote a book called *White House Pets*, which, come to think of it, is an excellent idea…

Dwight D. Eisenhower (1953–61) came to the White House with two dogs: a Weimaraner called Heidi and a Scottie named Spunky. Unfortunately, Heidi had little sense of etiquette and was repeatedly caught depositing her unique calling card on the brand-new carpet of the Diplomatic Room. Despite these mishaps, Eisenhower commented that 'Heidi is definitely an asset to life in the White House ... She is extremely affectionate and seemingly happy.' But it seems that as time went on, Heidi found life in the White House simply too stressful an atmosphere and she eventually retired happily to Eisenhower's farm.

As we have seen, some presidential families have practically had their own zoos at the White House: Calvin Coolidge kept more than twenty-five pets during his time in office, and Theodore Roosevelt more than forty. But perhaps the building's most famous animal-loving residents were John and Jackie Kennedy. Both had grown up with many pets, and they wanted to ensure the same for their two children, despite living in Washington. When they arrived at the White House in 1961, the First Lady immediately designed and built a play-yard for the couple's animals that included living spaces for Macaroni, their daughter Caroline's pony (see photo section), horses, rabbits, guinea pigs and sheep. It was located just under the President's West Wing Office and became a place for him to relax away from the strains of leadership. Other Kennedy animals included two parakeets named Marybelle and Bluebell, hamsters and, briefly, a cat, Tom Kitten, until it was discovered that the President was allergic. Tom – later renamed Tom Terrific – soon moved in with Kennedy's secretary, Mary Gallagher.

As Kelly notes, Caroline had enjoyed watching the film *Bambi* with her friends. After this, Jackie made enquiries about getting a deer to live on the White House lawn. Before she could make any arrangements, Jackie received two as gifts from the Irish

President Éamon de Valera. But like many of the deer's wilder White House predecessors, when it became clear they were not suited in terms of temperament to grazing on the lawn, the animals were sent to the Tisch Children's Zoo.

However, the dogs were the Kennedys' most famous animals. They included a Welsh terrier named Charlie, whose doggy uncle had played Asta in the 1934 film *The Thin Man*. Charlie swam in the White House pool while the President did his daily laps. Kennedy also requested that Charlie was always there to greet him from Marine One, the presidential helicopter, when it landed on the White House lawn.

Pushinka was the daughter of Strelka, one of the first dogs in space, and she was given to Caroline Kennedy by Nikita Krushchev, the leader of the Soviet Union, in 1961. The story goes that poor Pushinka was whisked to the Walter Reed Army Medical Center to undergo a battery of tests for any hidden microphones, germs or bombs. The US army denied this, but it was likely true given the highly tense atmosphere of the Cold War at this point. The Russians even gave Pushinka her own passport, which remains in the Kennedy family collection at the John F. Kennedy Presidential Library in Boston. Pushinka, which roughly translates as 'fluffy' in Russian, was a small, white mixed-breed dog. While writing to thank Khrushchev, JFK stated that Pushinka's 'flight from the Soviet Union to the United States was not as dramatic as that of her mother, nevertheless it was a long voyage and she stood it well … We both appreciate you remembering these matters in your busy life'. Pushinka is not referenced in memos and diary entries linked to the Cuban Missile Crisis, but it's clear from the historiography of the period that there were many aspects to the US–Russia relationship at the time, and perhaps the gift of a dog was one small factor in preventing nuclear annihilation.

At the height of the stand-off, Charlie, the terrier, was a regular visitor to the Oval Office and apparently Kennedy visibly relaxed while stroking him. He would return the dog to Traphes Bryant, a White House electrician, telling him, 'It's time to make some decisions.' Bryant went on to look after both the Johnson and Nixon dogs, too, and later wrote *Dog Days at the White House: The Outrageous Memoirs of the Presidential Kennel Keeper*.

Charlie and Pushinka had a litter of pups together. To find them homes, children were encouraged to write to the White House explaining why they would make the best owner for a puppy. One cheeky replier, who lost out after failing to include their address, promised to 'raise the dog to be a Democrat, and bite all Republicans'. The 'pupniks', as Kennedy christened them, were named Blackie, White Tips, Streaker and Butterfly.

Jacqueline was an accomplished equestrian, and her children loved horses too, although John Jr was allergic to horsehair, like his father. Caroline appeared with Macaroni on the cover of *Life* magazine in 1962, and the pony became something of a cheeky crowd favourite just as Fala and Laddie Boy had been. In 1962, he ate a bouquet of daffodils straight from the hands of Empress Farah Pahlavi, the visiting wife of the Iranian shah. At one stage, a Christmas card was created of Macaroni pulling the Kennedy kids around the White House lawn on a sleigh.

The Kennedys received many horses as gifts, but Jaqueline's 'favourite treasure' was Sardar, a bay gelding from the President of Pakistan, Ayub Khan. Sardar was not a horse without controversy, however. He was transported to the United States via the Military Air Transport Service, and a Congressman who had been refused permission to use the service remarked that Sardar 'must be a horse of unbridled influence'. Macaroni may have been a present from Lyndon Johnson, although this is debated. However, Vice-President Johnson did give Caroline a pony called Tex. The three-year-old gelding was a Yucatan Bay pony, brown with one black shoe. Tex and Macaroni grazed together on the White House lawn. There is a photo of Caroline on Macaroni being led by a Secret Service agent on the White House lawn in the photo section.

A Connemara pony called Leprechaun was another gift from de Valera. By this stage, the White House had implemented an unofficial no-pets-as-gifts policy, but as de Valera was a head of state an exception was made. Leprechaun was very tame and became known for nibbling President Kennedy. De Valera also presented the First Lady with a black and white cocker spaniel called Shannon, which came with its own gold shamrock-adorned collar. A German shepherd named Clipper was also given to Jackie, this time by her husband's father, Joseph Kennedy. The *Washington Post* reported in January 1963 that Mrs Kennedy had been seen in disguise walking Clipper, one of her favourites, outside the White House. As Hager notes, when veteran reporter Helen Thomas asked Jackie what Clipper liked to eat, she replied, 'Reporters.'

On a sadder note, Black Jack, a riderless horse, participated in the funerals of President Kennedy in 1963, Herbert Hoover in 1964 and Lyndon B. Johnson in 1973. During Kennedy's funeral, six white horses pulled the caisson which carried his coffin.

Black Jack was a well-known military horse; over the course of his life, he took part in over 1,000 full honour funerals for members of the US armed forces, most of which occurred at Arlington National Cemetery where Kennedy is buried. Black Jack was a Morgan/American quarter horse cross and only one of two horses in the history of the USA to receive full military honours for his service. When Black Jack retired in 1973, Mrs Kennedy bought him for the nation.

She kept only Shannon, the spaniel who was a gift from the Irish President, after her husband's assassination. The family's other dogs were sent to live with friends and colleagues because Jackie Kennedy's New York apartment was just not large enough to house so many pets. But the Kennedys' love of animals endures to this day; indeed in June 2025 the JFK Library in Boston established a six-month exhibition about presidential pets, tracing White House animals from George Washington to Joe Biden.

When he entered the White House after Kennedy's assassination, Lyndon Baines Johnson (1963–69) brought two dogs with him, called Him and Her. They were primarily his daughter Luci's dogs, but they became closely associated with LBJ as President. Him was the first dog to attend his master's presidential parade on Inauguration Day. Him also held the very first number in the recently implemented Washington DC dog tag system. It annoyed some in the feminist movement in the 1960s that Him was given the number one; they felt it wasn't a good look for Her being number two. The licensing department did not assist in dampening the fuss when they replied that this was correct anyway as Him was a male and therefore the first in the pecking order.

Johnson risked the wrath of dog lovers everywhere in 1964 when he lifted both Him and Her by their ears. Johnson tried to write this off as the usual behaviour with hunting dogs to ensure dogs were in 'good voice' and said that he had been pulling Him's ears since he was pup and that he 'seemed to like it'. However, the Associated Press photographer who took the snap, Francis Miller, reported that Him yelped at the time (see photo section). The President countered that 'it does them good to let them yelp'. There was uproar in response; the Humane Society of Texas staged a protest and one senator even brought up the ear-pulling incident during negotiations over the 1964 Civil Rights Act. Johnson apologised following the incident, bowing to the strength of public opinion even though he did not seem to feel that he had mistreated the dogs.

The *Life* magazine article itself read, 'Not many dogs have been privileged to shoo birds off the White House lawn, get underfoot at a cabinet meeting or mingle with dignitaries at a State Ball. Certainly no dogs in all the world have the Bouquet Room as their private boudoir.' Of Miller, the photographer, *Life* wrote:

> Too wise in the ways of puppies to believe that affection alone would produce good photographs, Miller stretched himself out on the White House lawn, alternately barked like a dog, tossed a bone in the air, plied the beagles with his Yummies, huffed into the harmonica and joggled the toy bird in his left hand. This left him free to shoot the cover with his right hand and his right eye.

Johnson once joked that one of his previous dogs, before he

became President, had been named Little Beagle Johnson because 'it's cheaper if we all have the same monogram'. This is a reference to many members of the Johnson family having the same initials, including his wife 'Lady Bird' Johnson (her real name was Claudia Alta) and their daughters Lynda Bird and Luci Baines.

One of Johnson's favourite pets was a mongrel that his daughter found wandering at a petrol station on Thanksgiving in 1966. Unable to locate the owner of the dog, Luci brought the animal the few short miles to the family ranch in Johnson City, Texas. She named him Yuki – Japanese for 'snow' – and presented the dog to her father the next year as a birthday gift. Yuki sat in Cabinet meetings and was known to inspect all guests, including top military personnel who would solemnly shake his paw – sometimes before shaking each other's hands. Yuki attended Luci's wedding, wearing a special jumper for the occasion. The President wanted Yuki front and centre in the photos, but Lady Bird drew the line at that. Looking back on the dog's life, Luci later reflected that 'the story of Yuki is part of history'.

In 1972, three years into his retirement, LBJ began dictating his memoirs about growing up in Texas and his love of dogs. The final vinyl, released in 1975, was called *Dogs Have Always Been My Friends: Lyndon Johnson Reminisces*. Hager notes Johnson's words about Yuki: 'He is the friendliest and the smartest and the most constant in his attention of all the dogs I have known … We always thought he was with the circus because he was so well-trained.' Yuki was also known for 'singing' along with LBJ in front of ambassadors and other distinguished guests. The pair singing together can be heard on the recording of *Reminisces*.

Having decided not to run for a second full term as the Vietnam crisis escalated, LBJ invited Republican contender Richard Nixon to the White House to discuss the ongoing war. Yuki, who had been in the meeting, followed Nixon onto his helicopter as he prepared to leave. Johnson rushed to pick up Yuki. Hager writes that, later, Nixon recalled joking to LBJ, 'I said I wanted your job, not your dog!'

Yuki was by Johnson's side when he died in 1973. As Johnson said in his memoirs, 'We've had many dogs through these years, and now we have Yuki. And I think they saved the best for the last.' LBJ became disliked and isolated due to the consequences of the Vietnam War, but his dogs were a solace, and when he came onto the White House lawn by helicopter, he always looked forward to being greeted by them, just as Kennedy had done before him.

Known as one of the most Machiavellian Presidents, Richard Nixon (1969–74) realised early on that animals and animal stories could be manipulated for political gain. It was when running for Vice-President in 1952, on the ticket with Eisenhower, that Nixon proved his mettle in this regard. Embroiled in a string of interlinked corruption and bribery scandals, Nixon gave a televised address on 23 September in a last-ditch attempt to save his reputation and career. This became known as the 'Checkers Speech' for his mention of the family pet. Sixty million Americans tuned in to hear him insist that he was not using donations for personal gain, that his family lived a modest lifestyle and

> one other thing I probably should tell you, because if we don't they'll probably be saying this about me too, we did get

something – a gift – after the election. A man down in Texas heard Pat [Nixon's wife] on the radio mention the fact that our two youngsters would like to have a dog. And, believe it or not, the day before we left on this campaign trip we got a message from Union Station in Baltimore saying they had a package for us. We went down to get it. You know what it was? It was a little cocker spaniel dog in a crate that he'd sent all the way from Texas. Black and white spotted. And our little girl – Tricia, the six-year-old – named it Checkers. And you know, the kids, like all kids, love the dog and I just want to say this right now, that regardless of what they say about it, we're gonna keep it.

And thus, Nixon's 'man of the people' image was established – helped in no small way by Checkers the dog. The speech saved his political run, with thousands of demands pouring into the Republican Party's headquarters that Nixon should stay on the ticket. Hager argues that 'this televised address changed America – politically and culturally – forever.'

The full truth was that Checkers was given to Nixon by a Texas traveling salesman named Louis Carrol. He had read an interview with the VP contender's wife in which she mentioned how their two daughters desperately wanted a dog and hurried to send a telegram offering one of the recently born puppies of his own cocker spaniel to the girls. As Nixon wrote in his 1962 book *Six Crises*, 'If it hadn't been for that broadcast, I never would have been around to run for the presidency'. His version of the story didn't quite match the facts, but what Nixon clearly knew was the value of such a tale – and Checkers – to his political ambitions.

Though she died in 1964, five years before Nixon was elected, and was never officially a White House pet, in many ways Checkers might as well have been. 23 September, the date of the speech in 1952, is now celebrated as National Dogs in Politics Day – or, sometimes, National Checkers Day.

When he finally made it to the White House, Nixon brought along his daughters' dogs Vicky, a French poodle, and Pasha, a Yorkshire terrier. He was then presented with another dog by his staff: an Irish setter puppy. Nixon called him King Timahoe, the latter part after the Irish village in which his ancestors lived. As for the 'King' part, Nixon explained, 'If he's the presidential dog, he will be treated like a king, won't he? … Even a President's dog gets the royal treatment!' But the royal connotations didn't catch on in republican America, so the pup was known as simply Timahoe. The Irish setter learned to shake hands with visitors and attended First Daughter Tricia Nixon's wedding on the White House lawn alongside Vicky and Pasha. All three dogs wore floral wreaths for the event.

When Nixon was re-elected for a second presidential term in a landslide victory in 1972, the *New York Times* quoted Traphes Bryant, the White House electrician who was still helping presidential families with their dogs, as saying, 'I'm sure one [photograph] of the President working at his desk, with the red setter keeping him company, was worth 10,000 votes.'

Nixon's daughter, Julie Nixon Eisenhower, loved the dog, writing a children's story, 'Pasha Passes By', which explored the adventures of the Yorkshire terrier. It was published in the New Year's edition of the *Saturday Evening Post* in 1974. Pasha had a lovely life, living with two friends in the heated presidential kennels in the grounds of the White House.

After Nixon was brought down by the Watergate scandal, Gerald Ford's administration (1974–77) tried to present a more wholesome image. Ford brought a Siamese cat, Chan, to the White House and was given a golden retriever puppy named Liberty by White House photographer David Kennerly. Images of Liberty became so popular that a special rubber stamp was made with Liberty's paw in order to 'autograph' those posted out by the White House to her fans.

Ford wrote in his 1979 memoir that when Kennerly first found Liberty, he made many efforts to keep quiet the fact the dog was intended for the President.

> That was fine, the owner said, but what was the name of David's friend?
>
> David said it was a surprise; he wanted to keep the name secret.
>
> 'We don't sell dogs that way,' the owner replied. 'We have to know if the dog is going to a good home.'
>
> 'The couple is friendly,' David said, 'They're middle-aged, and they live in a white house with a big yard and a fence around it. It's a lovely place.'
>
> 'Do they own or rent?' the owner asked.
>
> David thought for a minute. 'I guess you might call it public housing,' he said.

David ultimately came clean and plans were made to send the dog to the White House. She soon settled in. On one occasion, Ford took Liberty out to do her business in the middle of the night, but the doors of the White House locked behind him and the President had to make quite the commotion to alert staff that he and Liberty should be let back in.

In 1974, Ford discussed Liberty while addressing an audience of Philadelphia Republicans:

> One of those inquisitive reporters we have in Washington asked Susan who is going to take care of Liberty; who is going to feed her and groom her and take her out each night or every morning? And Susan did not hesitate one minute. She said 'of course it will be Dad'. So, I have this feeling – this is one Liberty that is going to cost me some of mine. But in a very broader sense, that is the true meaning of liberty. It comes with both privileges and obligations. Freedom, we all know, is seldom free.

Here, Ford was making his animal political: using Liberty the dog as a useful, universal symbol with which all his electorate would be familiar, to illustrate the broader idea of the nature of personal freedom and governance that went to the heart of the American republic.

In 1977, Jimmy Carter arrived in the White House with only one cat in tow, a Siamese called Misty Malarky Ying Yang, but soon his nine-year-old daughter Amy received a puppy as a gift from one of her teachers. Misty was not best pleased. The dog's name, Grits, came from Carter's election campaign slogan, 'Grits and Fritz in '76'. This was a play on Carter's southern roots and the nickname of his running mate Walter 'Fritz' Mondale. Amy adored Grits. The two would have sleepovers in the White House treehouse, a platform five feet off the ground in the shade of a huge tree. Unfortunately, Misty, who had been with the family since their time in Georgia, simply couldn't abide her new doggie brother, so Grits was eventually returned to his original owner.

Ronald Reagan (1981–89) was another President who did not hesitate to use dogs in photo opportunities to help bolster his wholesome image in the wake of criticism from the press about his physical robustness, age and health generally.

In December 1984, a small black Bouvier des Flandres puppy was given to First Lady Nancy Reagan by Kristen Ellis. Ellis, who was born with spina bifida, had been touring the United States campaigning for the charity March of Dimes, which raises money to help reduce infant mortality. The exact circumstances of how the Reagans ended up with Lucky are unknown. However, they knew little of the breed and were shocked that their small puppy grew up to be so big.

Hager writes, 'Lucky had a name which reinforced the optimistic "morning in America" theme of President Reagan's re-election campaign and captured the general "proud to be an American" spirit of 1980s patriotism.' Yet Lucky didn't last long in the White House, largely due to her energy and size. Lucky grew to over thirty kilos and the White House lawn became too small for her exercise needs. She was also known to have not been properly house-trained. An Associated Press reporter at one stage in Lucky's short time in the White House asked Nancy Reagan's press secretary if it was true that Lucky had soiled the Camp David carpet. Sheila Tate, the press secretary, replied, 'If I told you that, it would be an unauthorized leak.'

A photo of the huge dog sitting on Reagan's lap on Marine One (presumably crushing the President's knees) coupled with footage of Lucky dragging Reagan across the White House lawn, much to the amusement of Margaret Thatcher, meant the dog became more of a distraction than a pet. It also wasn't good for a President's image to have the large, bounding, enthusiastic but perhaps not the most sophisticated animal causing mayhem in the White House and beyond. Lucky was a case of a political animal that, while loved, was not a good addition to his master's political image. Lucky was moved to the Reagans' California ranch in 1985 after just five months at the White House.

Though Lucky did not achieve the iconic status of some of her predecessors, she did have a paw in the establishing of the Presidential Pet Museum. Lucky's groomer, Claire McLean, had kept some of the dog's fur, which she passed on to her mother. McLean's mother then incorporated the fur into a painting of Lucky. Claire McLean felt the portrait was worth preserving and over the next two decades built the collections of the museum. Lucky's portrait remains at the Presidential Pet Museum to this day, alongside many hundreds of other artefacts.

Ronald Reagan knew the publicity potential in having a dog, so he made sure that their next pup would be less of a handful. Rex the King Charles spaniel arrived on Christmas 1985 as a gift for the First Lady. The President had acquired the dog from right-wing commentator William F. Buckley Jr. The National Children's Museum in Washington DC commissioned a doghouse for Rex designed by Theo Hayes, who was married to a descendant of President Rutherford B. Hayes. She described it as

> very colonial … White clapboard with a cedar shingle roof. I didn't do it feminine or prissy. It's not as if I was doing it for

a French poodle or a chihuahua. There are draperies of red fabric … and on the wall are pictures of Ron and Nancy in acrylic frames.

At the end of Reagan's administration, Rex joined his master in Hollywood and enjoyed all the trappings of a presidential retirement by the side of the pool in Bel Air, California, as Kelly notes in *Presidential Pets*.

In 1989, George and Barbara Bush arrived at the White House with an English springer spaniel named Millie. When she had puppies they gave one, Spot Fletcher (later shortened to Spotty), to their son. When George Jr returned to the White House as President in 2001, Spot became the only dog to live there during non-consecutive terms.

Once, Millie was rather meanly described as 'homely' and 'the ugliest dog in Washington' by John Sansing in *Washingtonian* magazine. President Bush replied with grace: 'Imagine picking on a guy's dog.' Jack Limpert, the magazine's editor, apologised and sent treats as a peace offering, to which the President responded, 'Not to worry! Millie, you see, likes publicity. Arf, arf for the dog biscuits.' Millie even appeared as a character on the sitcoms *Wings* and *Murphy Brown*, as Hager notes, and the Bushes and Millie were all satirised in a famous episode of *The Simpsons*. *Millie's Book: As Dictated to Barbara Bush*, earned the First Lady a staggering $1.1 million in royalties in its first year of publication alone.

An earlier book 'slightly edited by Barbara Bush', titled *C. Fred's Story: A Dog's Life*, was published in 1984 when George H. W. Bush was Vice-President. C. Fred was named after Bush's business partner and friend C. Fred Chambers. The book recounts the Bushes' adventures during George's varied career as a member of the House of Representatives, ambassador to the United Nations, US ambassador to China, CIA director and then Vice-President, via Washington, Houston, Texas and Beijing. George H. W. Bush's biographer Curt Smith writes in his presidential biography *George H. W. Bush: Character at the Core* that Barbara Bush is cast in the book in a 'sympathetic, down-home, dog and child loving light' leading to a 'bond over the next third of a century between Mrs. Bush and America that was improbable, even phenomenal'. The historian Katherine A. S. Sibley argues that the book was intended as a 'subtle way to get to know the second family' as well as being an instrument in Barbara Bush's campaign to increase childhood literacy.

At the 2004 press secretaries' panel discussion at the George Bush Presidential Library, Hager notes that Anna Perez, Barbara Bush's press secretary, stated that it was easy to stay on the First Lady's good side: 'Don't mess with her man. Don't mess with her kids. And don't mess with her dog.'

Another of Millie's six pups was Ranger. When Ranger rapidly gained weight, the President was widely mocked for an unintentionally hilarious memo he sent White House staff.

IMPORTANT ANNOUNCEMENT
February 6, 1992
THIS IS AN ALL POINTS BULLETIN FROM THE PRESIDENT
SUBJECT: MY DOG 'RANGER'

Recently Ranger was put on a weight-reduction program.

Either that program succeeds or we enter Ranger in the Houston Fat Stock Show as a Prime Hereford.

All offices should take a formal 'pledge' that reads as follows: 'WE AGREE NOT TO FEED RANGER. WE WILL NOT GIVE HIM BISCUITS. WE WILL NOT GIVE HIM FOOD OF ANY KIND.'

In addition, Ranger's 'access' is hereby restricted. He has been told not to wander the corridors without an escort. This applies to the East and West Wings, to the Residence from the 3rd floor to the very, very bottom basement.

Although Ranger will still be permitted to roam at Camp David, the Camp David staff including Marines, Naval Personnel, All Civilians and Kids are specifically instructed to 'rat' on anyone seen feeding Ranger.

Ranger has been asked to wear a 'Do not feed me' badge in addition to his ID.

I will, of course, report on Ranger's fight against obesity. Right now he looks like a blimp, a nice friendly appealing blimp, but a blimp.

We Need Your Help – All hands, please help.

FROM THE PRESIDENT

Bush made another faux pas on the re-election trail in 1992 by saying, 'My dog Millie knows more about foreign policy than those two bozos.' Unfortunately for him the 'bozos' in question were Bill Clinton and Al Gore, who duly trounced him. After a long and happy life, Millie passed away in 1997 at the age of twelve.

Many cat owners will attest to the Cat Distribution System, a mysterious phenomenon through which cats seem to choose us, rather than the other way round. In 1991, Bill Clinton was governor of Arkansas and living with his family in the gubernatorial mansion in the state capitol, Little Rock. His daughter, Chelsea, was about to start her piano lesson when she spotted two kittens her teacher had been trying to reunite with their mother. When Chelsea reached out to the kittens, one jumped into her arms. Socks, as he was later named, instantly became a Clinton (see photo section). A local animal shelter helped Socks's brother find a good home elsewhere.

Clinton (1993–2001) brought Socks with him to the White House despite being allergic to cats. Socks proved very popular with the public and indeed the White House reporters, who would give Socks catnip, attempting to get the best angles for photographs. He was totally unfazed by the attention, though the press pack became so fond of him that eventually the Clintons had to ask them not to handle their cat.

Hager notes that Socks appeared in numerous guises. He was interviewed as a *Muppet* version of himself on *Larry King Live* during an April Fool's Day episode hosted by Kermit the Frog and starred in an unreleased Super Nintendo video game called *Socks the Cat Rocks the Hill*. An animated Socks character was also used by the Clinton administration on their 'White House for Kids' website.

Republican representative Dan Burton made a bid to incite scandal by querying why public funds were being used to reply to Socks's fan mail from children. Many former Presidents had of course done much the same thing, such as Gerald Ford's 'paw-tographs' of Liberty, as Hager observes. The smear campaign that Burton likely hoped to ignite failed dramatically as no one had a bad word to say about Socks the superstar. And his fans needed their replies.

Four years into their White House term, the Clintons adopted Buddy, a chocolate-coloured Labrador retriever, to help fill the void left when their daughter Chelsea left for Stanford University in California. The puppy was donated by the Wild Goose Kennels of Maryland, which had originally named him Teddy, after Theodore Roosevelt. Thousands sent in ideas for names, but 'Buddy' was eventually chosen in honour of the President's recently deceased great-uncle, Henry Oren 'Buddy' Grisham, a mentor to Bill and a dog trainer for five decades.

Shortly after Buddy's name was revealed to the public, and just as the First Lady's press secretary was answering a question on the very matter of how Socks and Buddy got along, Socks took a swipe at Buddy on the South Lawn and the pair had to be separated. Eventually, Buddy started to appreciate Socks and tried to make peace, but Socks never apparently reciprocated. Hager records that Bill Clinton notoriously once joked that he had found it easier negotiating peace between Israelis and Palestinians than between Socks and Buddy.

Buddy's sleeping spot of choice was behind the President's desk in the Oval Office, and he was known to pester Clinton incessantly until the President played with him and his ball on the lawn – animals have their priorities straight. Towards the end of their time at the White House, Hillary Clinton edited a children's book titled *Dear Socks, Dear Buddy: Kids' letters to the First Pets*. Like other First Ladies before her, Clinton chose a good cause to receive the proceeds from the book, in this case the National Parks Foundation.

On leaving office, Buddy went with the Clintons to their New

York property. Tragically, Buddy was killed in a road accident while the Clintons were away. Socks was given to Betty Currie, the President's personal secretary, whom the cat adored. They lived in Washington DC's neighbouring state of Maryland until Socks's death from cancer in 2009 at over twenty years old. He was certainly the most famous moggy to ever grace 1600 Pennsylvania Avenue.

George W. Bush's (2001–09) Scottish terrier Barney was a Christmas gift to the President-elect from his wife Laura in 2000. Bush considered him 'the son I never had'. Barney entertained and amused the American – and world – public through his *Barney Cam* videos. Hager writes that Barney 'became a symbolic emotional support animal for a confused and anxious populace' during a troubling time in American history following 9/11 and with war raging in Afghanistan and Iraq.

The idea for the *Barney Cam* clips came from the White House internet director Jimmy Orr in 2002 as a way of showcasing the Christmas decorations online. Inspired by that year's theme of 'All Creatures Great and Small', Orr and his colleagues pitched the idea of Barney running around the White House with a camera on his head. Press secretary Ari Fleischer declared the idea to be 'awesome!' The press team set about acquiring a lipstick-size camera, a mini recording device they planned to attach to the dog's collar. However, Barney had never worn, or indeed needed, a collar until then, so when they tried to put one on, his immediate reaction was to roll around the floor and howl; clearly that was not going to work.

The next plan was a basic one: simply crouching down and following Barney around at his own level. Obviously. This gave a 'dog's-eye view' of the festive decor. *Barney Cam* became very popular incredibly quickly after being launched at the Children's National Medical Center, and broadcast simultaneously by several TV networks. It quickly not only became the item on the White House website with the largest number of views – over 24 million in the first days alone – but was followed by six sequels. David Almacy was the White House internet director in the latter stages of the Bush administration. Hager notes that Almacy spoke later about becoming emotional as he saw the extent to which the *Barney Cam* videos offered the children in hospital a welcome distraction from their very serious health conditions. Soon, many in the White House were appearing in *Barney Cam*. This even included the President himself, who popped up to extol the virtues of hard work to the dour Scottie.

The second instalment, *Barney Cam II: Barney Reloaded*, was described thus by the *New York Times*: 'The plot of the video is more complex than last year's video, which had no plot.' Celebrity guests lined up to be featured, including Olympic gold medallists Michael Phelps and Nastia Liukin. Barney's Christmas videos featured cameos from UK Prime Minister Tony Blair, Bush adviser Karl Rove, as well as country singers Dolly Parton and Alan Jackson.

In the 2008 *Barney Cam* Christmas greeting, the last in the series, the First Family's Scottish terrier scampers amid the White House's red, white and blue holiday decorations before retiring for a nap and dreaming of himself as an athlete. Barney is shown in cutout animation as an Olympic pole vaulter, swimmer and synchronised diver with fellow terrier Miss Beazley, both in red swimsuits. The dream concludes with Barney sinking the final putt to secure the US Ryder Cup, with the entire Ryder Cup team chanting his name.

After Bush left office, he, his wife, Laura, and their daughters, Jenna and Barbara, recorded a video reminiscing about their time together in the White House with Barney, before sending him off to hang Christmas decorations and to nap.

But not everyone was so keen on Barney. Senior White House adviser Karl Rove remarked shortly after his resignation that the dog was 'a lump'. Barney was also criticised by Russian President Vladimir Putin: he felt that a world leader should own large, robust dogs, not smaller breeds such as the Scottish terrier. At one stage, when Putin introduced Bush to Koni, his black Labrador, Putin is reported to have remarked that Koni is 'bigger, tougher, stronger, faster, meaner than Barney'.

Despite his loving and playful nature, Barney wasn't afraid to bare his teeth. In November 2008, Barney bit the finger of Jon Decker, a Reuters reporter. Barney had also bitten Boston Celtics' public relations director Heather Walker on the wrist the month before, breaking the skin and drawing blood, but the incident was not reported until after the presidential election on 4 November that year. Laura Bush's spokesperson joked afterwards that 'I think it was his way of saying he was done with the paparazzi'.

For Christmas 2004, a second Scottie, the aforementioned Miss Beazley, was added to the Bush stable, this time a present from the President to the First Lady. Barney and Miss Beazley were portrayed as rivals for the cameras; however, in reality they were not only uncle and niece but also best dog friends. When

Miss Beazley died in 2014, President Bush commented that 'even though he [Barney] got all the attention, she never held a grudge against him'.

While Barney and Miss Beazley took most of the pet spotlight, a less well-known member of the menagerie was the Bushes' much-loved cat India, a solid black American shorthair. Arriving at the Texas governor's mansion as a kitten in 1991, India largely stayed out of the limelight, although she did make occasional appearances in the *Barney Cam* videos. When the cat died in January 2009 at the grand age of eighteen, a spokesman for Laura Bush said, 'India was a beloved member of the Bush family for almost two decades. She will be greatly missed.'

Barney sadly crossed the rainbow bridge to doggy heaven in 2013, having served every day of George W. Bush's time at the White House. He was twelve and a half years old. Paying tribute, his dad wrote:

> Laura and I are sad to announce that our Scottish terrier, Barney, has passed away. The little fellow had been suffering from lymphoma and, after twelve and a half years of life, his body could not fight off the illness. Barney and I enjoyed the outdoors. He loved to accompany me when I fished for bass at the ranch. He was a fierce armadillo hunter. At Camp David, his favorite activity was chasing golf balls on the chipping green. Barney guarded the South Lawn entrance of the White House as if he were a Secret Service agent. He wandered the halls of the West Wing looking for treats from his many friends. He starred in *Barney Cam* and gave the American people Christmas tours of the White House. Barney greeted

Queens, Heads of State, and Prime Ministers. He was always polite and never jumped in their laps. Barney was by my side during our eight years in the White House. He never discussed politics and was always a faithful friend. Laura and I will miss our pal.

CHAPTER FIVE

CONTEMPORARY PRESIDENTIAL PETS

It was during my time working as a producer for the BBC in the final days of George W. Bush's presidency that I visited the White House, although sadly I didn't get to meet his dogs. As both a workplace and a home, the White House is an incredible building and a wonderful playground for a pet. I did get to see the press room on my visit, though, thanks to the generosity of a more senior journalist, the long-serving White House correspondent Connie Lawn, who died in 2018.

Various pets over the years 'gave' press conferences in the world-famous room, which have always been popular with the press and public. What is less well known is that the press room is built on top of what was once a swimming pool that had been installed by John F. Kennedy. His successor, Richard Nixon, had it turned into a press room in the late 1960s to accommodate the growing demand for television news. A floor was put in on top of the old pool, leaving a room below that now houses reporters' offices and much of the equipment and miles of wiring required by broadcasters. The tiles are still visible down there, and you can even sign your name – I put mine next to where U2 frontman Bono had scrawled his.

In his acceptance speech on the night of 4 November 2008,

Barack Obama, who went on to serve as President from 2009 to 2017, promised more than just hope for the American nation. Addressing his daughters Sasha and Malia, then seven and ten years old respectively, Obama declared, 'I love you both more than you can imagine. You have earned the puppy that is coming with us!' Malia, however, was allergic to some dogs, so the Obama family eventually settled on a Portuguese water dog, which are a hypoallergenic breed. Named Bo, the puppy arrived at the White House in April of 2009, about three months after the Obamas. It might be easy to presume Bo's name was created from the President's initials, but, as Hager points out, Michelle Obama's late father, Fraser Robinson III, had the nickname 'Diddley', after rock 'n' roll pioneer Bo Diddley.

Bo was given to the family by Senator Ted Kennedy of Massachusetts, the brother of former President. Ted Kennedy himself owned water dogs, so he knew the breed and its advantages well. When he brought his pet Splash into work he complained about Splash being restricted from the Senate floor: 'He's troubled by that. He says he behaves a lot better than most senators.' On the Hill, Kennedy's Senate office interns were often tasked with taking his dogs for walks along the streets and parks of Washington DC, including the less-than-glamorous duty of cleaning up after them.

Dana Lewis, a former personal aide to the First Lady, stated that Bo 'knew he was an Obama. He could always turn it on in public.' Bo was an exceptionally intelligent dog who knew how to work the White House elevator with his paws and was known to wander the mansion looking for staffers to give him treats, which they always did. As well as the usual obedience training many dogs receive, he was trained as a comfort animal and visited children and veterans in hospital. In his 2020 memoir, *A Promised Land*, Obama wrote:

> Bo gave me an added excuse to put off my evening paperwork and join my family on meandering after-dinner walks around the South Lawn. It was during those moments – with the light fading into streaks of purple and gold, Michelle smiling and squeezing my hand as Bo bounded in and out of the bushes with the girls giving chase – that I felt normal and whole and as lucky as any man has a right to expect.

In August 2013, a second Portuguese water dog joined the First Family. Michelle felt that Sunny would be 'the perfect little sister for Bo'. But the life of a presidential pet is not without its perils. In January 2016, the Secret Service arrested a man claiming to be both Jesus and the love child of JFK and Marilyn Monroe, who had driven from North Dakota to kidnap either Bo or Sunny.

Happily, Bo remained with the family long after they left the White House before finally succumbing to cancer in 2021 at the ripe old age of thirteen. Obama wrote on Twitter at the time, 'He tolerated all the fuss that came with being in the White House, had a big bark but no bite, loved to jump in the pool in the summer, was unflappable with children, lived for scraps around the dinner table, and had great hair.'

Obama's opponent for the presidency in the 2012 election, Mitt Romney, fared less well when it came to tales of his pet. In June 2007, Neil Swidey reported in the *Boston Globe* that, back in 1983,

Romney had placed his family's Irish setter, Seamus, in a carrier on top of the family Chevrolet Caprice station wagon while the family made a twelve-hour journey to Ontario for a holiday. Seamus got diarrhoea during the trip, which a number of veterinarians later noted may have indicated he was highly stressed. But Romney simply washed the dog down at a service station during a pit stop and put him back up on the roof of the car for the remainder of the 650-mile journey. He was criticised for his treatment of Seamus during his presidential campaigns in 2008 and 2012. Unsurprisingly, many animal lovers and animal rights organisations, such as PETA, were outraged. Romney defended his actions and said he had constructed a windshield for Seamus.

Donald Trump (2017–21 and 2025–present) famously has had no animals in the White House. When he was first elected President, he became the first Oval Office resident since Harry Truman, nearly fifty years earlier, not to have had a dog upon (or shortly after) entering the White House; in fact, the Trumps are the first presidential family in modern times not to have a pet of any kind.

Speaking at a campaign rally in El Paso, Texas, Trump remarked, 'You do love your dogs, don't you? I wouldn't mind having one, honestly, but I don't have any time. How would I look walking a dog on the White House lawn? Would that be right?' He then shook his head as the crowd agreed that it would not be. He continued on his theme: 'I don't know. Feels a little phony, phony to me. A lot of people say, "Oh, you should get a dog", "Why?" "It's good politically." I said, "Look, that's not the relationship I have with my people."'

At that point someone in the crowd shouted, 'Obama had a dog!' to which Trump replied, laughing, 'Yeah, Obama had a dog, you're right!' In the same speech, Trump also praised German shepherd dogs for their 'unbelievable' ability to sniff out drugs.

In a 2019 article on ABC News, Meridith McGraw notes that Trump has often used comparisons to dogs as an insult. His enemies have 'choked like a dog', 'barked like a dog', 'sweated like a dog', 'lied like a dog', have been 'dumped like a dog' or were 'fired like a dog'. Trump has frequently made criticisms relating negative behaviour to canine traits: in September 2024, Trump falsely accused Haitian immigrants in Ohio of eating dogs and cats. He seems to use animal imagery in negative contexts, while not being a fan of pets himself.

During the 2024 presidential election, comments surfaced from a 2021 speech given by Trump's running mate J. D. Vance in which he called Democratic politicians 'a bunch of childless cat ladies with miserable lives'. The speech was made to a conservative organisation called the Intercollegiate Studies Institute. In a subsequent interview with the journalist Megyn Kelly in July 2024, Vance said he was being sarcastic but 'the substance of what I said, Megyn – I'm sorry, it's true'. He also denied he was against people who did not have children, or against people who couldn't have children for medical or biological reasons.

Trump did, however, welcome a dog as a guest to the Executive Mansion in November 2019. Conan was a Belgian Malinois trained and handled by US military personnel and had been injured in the raid that led to the death of Islamic State leader Abu Bakr al-Baghdadi.

Trump told reporters that Conan was a 'tough cookie … beautiful … the ultimate fighter, ultimate everything'. He congratulated Conan in a series of tweets, awarding the dog a plaque and a medal. As Hager points out, First Spouses can have a large influence when it comes to animals in the White House. Melania, America's First Lady, was asked if she wanted to adopt Conan for her then thirteen-year-old son Barron, but, as the *Washington Post* reported, 'she appeared to decline'.

Other members of the Trump family are definitely animal lovers. Lara Trump, the President's daughter-in-law, helped develop legislation to prevent animal cruelty and worked on the successful campaign to ban greyhound racing in Florida. Trump's daughter Ivanka has a white pomsky dog called Winter, who sometimes features on her social media channels.

Trump announced at the 2025 State of the Union that a wildlife reserve was to be renamed after a murdered young girl who had loved animals. He told Congress:

> One thing I have learned about Jocelyn is that she loved animals so much. She loved nature. Across Galveston Bay from where Jocelyn lived in Houston, you will find a magnificent national wildlife refuge, a pristine, peaceful, 34,000-acre sanctuary for all of God's creatures on the edge of the Gulf of America. Alexis, [Jocelyn's mother] moments ago, I formally renamed that refuge in loving memory of your beautiful daughter, Jocelyn.

Mike Pence, Trump's first Vice-President, was more pet-oriented.

He arrived at the White House with two cats, a snake, an Australian shepherd called Harley (a gift from his wife, though he had actually asked for a motorbike) and, most famously, his daughter Charlotte's pet rabbit Marlon Bundo.

The bunny soon had his own Instagram account with thousands of followers. A children's book, *Marlon Bundo's A Day in the Life of the Vice-President*, was written by Charlotte and illustrated by her mother, Karen. In it, Marlon followed 'Grampa Pence' through a routine workday. The money raised funded cancer and anti-human-trafficking charities. A 'rival' book was then written by a staff writer on the satirical TV programme *Last Week Tonight* with John Oliver. Jill Twiss wrote *A Day in the Life of Marlon Bundo*, a progressive's take on Marlon's story in which Marlon falls in love with another male rabbit named Wesley. Proceeds from this book, which sold 600,000 copies, went to AIDS and LGBT charities. While the Pence family's original book only sold 32,000 copies, ultimately many charities benefited from Marlon's adventures.

The 'Second Rabbit' was by far the most famous animal of Trump's first term, though the family dog Harley also got a look-in. The *Washington Post* ruminated on the most appropriate way to address the pooch: 'Pence spokesman Marc Lotter deemed Harley the Nation's "Second Dog", which seemed a bit unfair. There is no First Dog, after all. And if the rabbit is BOTUS, shouldn't Harley be DOTUS?'

Joe Biden acquired Champ Biden, a German shepherd while serving as Vice-President to Barack Obama. In late 2018 Major, another German shepherd, joined the family and they went on to the White House together not as Second but as First Dogs following Biden's presidential victory over Trump in 2020.

During Trump's re-election campaign in 2020, a group called 'Dog Lovers for Joe' released a short advertisement contrasting animal-loving Joe with a dogless Trump. The intention was to highlight Trump's presidency as an 'aberration' and how it was essential to elect Biden to restore 'normalcy'. The organisation's website argued:

> Right now is the first time in over 100 years there hasn't been a dog in the White House and it shows. Science shows that dogs make us more compassionate, more friendly, healthier and happier. In fact, according to a recent study published in *The Guardian*, 'animal therapy helps to develop problem-solving skills, empathy, attention to the needs of others, a sense of responsibility and a way of channelling aggressive thoughts among individuals who have proved hard to reach with conventional psychiatric drugs and talking therapies'. In other words, vote for Joe – he's a dog guy.

The ad itself featured photos of recent Presidents with their dogs, including Clinton, Bush and Obama, accompanied by a strapline reading, 'Trump is the first President without a dog in the White House in over a century.' A clip follows of Trump at the El Paso rally when he asked, 'How would I look walking a dog on the White House lawn?' Then shaking his head while the crowd cheers. A photo of Biden holding Champ then appears, ending with the strapline 'Choose your humans wisely.'

With Biden's election victory, Major became the first rescue dog to live in the White House. Born in 2018, he was fostered and then adopted from the Delaware Humane Association (DHA) in Biden's home state. On 17 January 2021, three days before the official presidential inauguration, Pumpkin Pet Insurance and the DHA held a virtual 'indoguration' for Major. The singer Josh Groban performed at the event, which was hosted by NBC *Today* correspondent Jill Martin. The ceremony was watched by over 100,000 people online and it raised $202,000 for the DHA.

In 2021, First Lady Jill Biden appeared with Champ and Major on Animal Planet's annual *Puppy Bowl*, which broadcasts during the Superbowl and provides a furry element to the big sports event. She and the dogs appeared in a thirty-second public service announcement in which she asked Americans to wear masks while out in public. She showed the doggies as she stated, 'We owe it to them to stay healthy.' As Hager says, this makes the pair of dogs 'a new type of First Pet, born in an era of social media and viral sensations – presidential pets as influencers'.

Champ and Major did not complete their White House existence entirely without scandal. As with many others before them, they did not adjust well to the stressful environment of their surroundings. This stress often manifested itself in the dogs lashing out at strangers. Major bit a Secret Service agent and a National Park Service employee on two separate occasions early in Biden's presidency. Though the wounds were superficial and not at all serious – not even drawing blood – Major was sent for additional correctional and behaviour training. In March 2021, *Saturday Night Live* spoofed the biting incidents, showing Kamala Harris's husband Doug Emhoff (played by Martin Short) being attacked by Major during a Passover dinner.

In August 2021 the conservative watchdog, Judicial Watch, obtained a series of emails showing that Major had been involved in many more biting incidents than had previously been disclosed. Though all the injuries were minor, the dog's behaviour was clearly starting to become a problem. The White House insisted Major had not bitten anyone since his behaviour training, but ultimately, in December 2021, the White House announced that 'it would be safest for Major to live in a quieter environment', and he went to live with family friends of the Bidens.

Major's grief was also perhaps a factor in his aggression, particularly after Champ had died earlier that year at the Bidens' Delaware home at the age of thirteen. In a statement, the First Lady wrote, 'Our hearts are heavy today … In our most joyful moments and in our most grief-stricken days, he was there with us, sensitive to our every unspoken feeling and emotion. We love our sweet, good boy and will miss him always.'

Perhaps due to the increased glare of the social media age, the Biden dogs frequently found themselves in the headlines. Prior to Biden's inauguration, the press reported that the future President fractured his foot while playing with Major. Major and Champ were often photographed as a pair. For Christmas, Jill Biden released a video of the two dogs, highlighting their different personalities: a stoic and subdued Champ, accompanied by an energetic and playful Major.

In December 2021, the Bidens, ever the dog-loving family, accepted a gift from the President's brother James and his wife

Sara: Commander, a three-month-old German shepherd puppy. Though not a rescue animal, he nonetheless took to his pawlitical duties with the same energy as his shelter adoptee friends. Commander posed for official photos, which Biden happily shared with patients at the Children's National Medical Center on Christmas Eve. On Christmas Day, the puppy was seen with the presidential couple in a virtual event thanking US military personnel worldwide for their work. But Commander was another biter, so he, too, was rehomed in 2023. One of the victims, various media reported at the time, required hospital treatment for the injury. CNN later calculated that there had been twenty-four incidents of Commander biting someone.

The other Biden animal was Willow the tabby cat, who arrived in 2022 after Commander and Major had been safely rehomed. Willow had first come to the attention of the First Lady during a 2020 election campaign stop at a farm. Jill Biden explained in an interview that the American shorthair tabby had been living with a foster family and that she had grown attached to the cat. Her team asked Rick Telesz, Willow's former owner, if Jill could adopt Willow from him, and she came to live at the White House.

The guru when it comes to presidential pets in this area – the top dog as it were – is the aforementioned Andrew Hager. As a strong advocate of rescue animals himself, he has observed an increasing number of White House animals are from rescue shelters. Having studied presidential pets for years, Hager has established that, as important as funny stories of pets' antics and their lovely photos and portraits are, for many Presidents there are two very serious roles that their pets play: the comfort they bring under stress and the way their image powerfully 'softens' or 'humanises' their owners. With US politics being highly divisive – and increasingly so – seeing how a top politician interacts with their pet can give voters a political insight beyond the imagery or superficial charm displayed in election campaigns.

As Hager writes, Americans have a strong historical connection to their pets. He suggested that early colonists brought a 'canine culture' with them when they travelled to the New World. He evidences how they frequently put adverts in papers trying to locate lost dogs and wrote public tributes to them on their animals' passing, which demonstrates that there was a strand of pet appreciation amongst early colonists that went above regarding animals as simply being useful to humans. The foundation has remained to this day.

Hager also mentions how the stories of dogs, cats or other animals sleeping in the same bed as the Presidents or sharing the Oval Office with them contributed to the perception of pets being full family members, a view that remains to this day.

'Americans as a whole', Hager writes, 'are both cat *and* dog people, and we have been for some time,' but of course dogs are more obedient and generally sit for political photo opportunities with less hassle. It is clear a presidential pet choice is not just out of circumstance but utility too.

Although Trump made it twice to the White House without a pet, there is no doubt that – similarly to the UK – the US is a nation of animal lovers with a particular fondness for dogs. The US Constitution requires Trump to leave the White House in 2029, and his would-be successors will perhaps benefit from noting that the American Veterinary Medical Association calculates that 68 per cent of all Americans own a pet, and 48.5 per cent own more than one.

For many Presidents throughout American history, presidential pets have proven to not only have been companions, even friends, but also political assets.

PART III

THE POLITICAL ANIMALS OF WHITEHALL

CHAPTER SIX

PALMERSTON AT THE FOREIGN OFFICE

When Sir Simon McDonald became the top civil servant at the Foreign Office in 2015, he thought times had changed since he joined the institution three decades previously. Various events had shaken the global kaleidoscope: the Berlin Wall had fallen, the Twin Towers had been hit and apartheid had ended in South Africa. These three incidents were almost unthinkable when McDonald first entered the Foreign Office building, tucked away on King Charles Street off Whitehall. But one aspect remained stubbornly the same: the mice and rats.

In an interview for *Political Animals*, McDonald, now a member of the House of Lords, recalls his first days leading the Foreign Office. He decided to write a blog for his civil servants around the world. 'I was comparing the office as a building in 2015 with the office as a building in 1982 when I joined, and I said, basically, it's recognisable, but better. And one way it's better is we don't have rats and mice running around the joint any more.'

Replies from Foreign Office civil servants came thick and fast. 'There was a deluge of commentary from remote parts of King Charles Street saying, "Well, it may be all right in your corner office but, up here, we still have a problem,"' says McDonald. 'And in this correspondence, someone suggested, "Why don't you get an office cat?"' So he did.

'Of course, we knew about Larry, but the inspiration was the vermin problem in the Foreign Office.' Larry had spent the previous four years on Downing Street lazing around and not catching many mice. Nonetheless, not every cat is as lazy as Larry and some do quite enjoy hunting and keeping workplaces and homes free from vermin.

As with many civil service procurement processes, obtaining a cat was not without obstacles, sign-offs from various jobsworthsian figures and a whole lot of paperwork, even for the Foreign Office's most senior civil servant. 'It was only because I was Permanent Secretary that I was able to overcome the numerous bureaucratic hurdles,' says McDonald. The red tape duly cut through, the time had come for McDonald and his acolytes to get down to the business of recruiting the mouser in question.

> I had a little office, including a private secretary and two assistant private secretaries, and one of them had the task of recruiting a mouser.
>
> There was a job spec, and the most important thing was that the cat should be a proper mouser. I don't want to besmirch Larry's reputation, but we thought we needed to be upfront about the key professional qualification. And second, the cat had to be able to cope with lots of attention. The people at Battersea Dogs & Cats Home knew what we were looking for, and they were extremely understanding and accommodating.

Less accommodating were some inside the civil service, who seemed determined to put up obstacles to the Foreign Office having a cat. 'Health and safety, the estate people, animal welfare people… there were many hurdles to jump,' explains McDonald. 'And the final thing was insurance, because what if he's responsible for an accident, or what if someone gets ill?' The hurdles were eventually overcome and Palmerston was the result. The black and white cat was acquired in spring 2016 – like Larry, from Battersea Dogs & Cats Home. Like so many of the beautiful rescue cats who come to such centres, Palmerston had been found on the streets of London, underweight, hungry and with no microchip. Cared for brilliantly by Battersea, he was soon ready for his new home. Shortly after arriving at the Foreign Office, Palmerston (with help) set up a JustGiving page for the charity, which raised over £3,000, giving something back to those who had rescued him, prepared him for adoption and found him his new home.

Buzzfeed journalist Emily Ashton penned many a story about Palmerston and the other Westminster cats, including one tale gained as the result of a freedom of information request to the Foreign Office by cat fans. Ashton revealed that Battersea originally gave Palmerston the name Leonard. Incidentally, Ashton is now a civil servant in the Department of Health, which is, sadly, at the time of writing, without a cat of its own (come on Emily, sort it out!). Ashton also revealed it was McDonald who changed the cat's name to Palmerston.

Henry John Temple, the third Viscount Palmerston, was Foreign Secretary on three occasions and dominated British foreign policy between 1830 and 1865 when Britain was at the height of its imperial power. He was Prime Minister for most of a decade, too. Palmerston was the longest-serving Foreign Secretary and one of the most influential in history. 'No other names were considered,' confirmed the Foreign Office to Buzzfeed. The Freedom of Information request also revealed that Larry 'gave' Palmerston a gift of a toy mouse and a packet of Dreamies soon after his arrival.

Palmerston quickly made a big impression and even 'wrote' for the internal news email of the Foreign Office on his first day. In it, he referenced Rocco, then Foreign Office minister Hugo Swire's dog, who was frequently brought into the King Charles Street offices:

> Wow, it's hard to believe that it's just a few weeks since I was scurrying inside the bins on the backstreets of London looking for my next meal. I'm one of the lucky strays – some kindly folk at Battersea Dogs & Cats home offered me some accommodation for a couple of weeks and suddenly I'm living, working and dining in one of the Great Offices of State.
>
> I was completely overwhelmed upon my arrival and wasn't expecting crowds of paparazzi to be waiting for me. After a quick photocall outside the building it was time to meet my new friends and colleagues in Simon McDonald's office. But there was no time to rest on my first day. After giving every nook and cranny of Simon's office a thorough inspection, it was back to media duties and my first interview with Buzzfeed.
>
> Then time for training. After Simon and his colleagues put me through my paces with pieces of string and various replica rodents – I think I'm finally ready for the massive mouse challenge ahead. Clearly my objectives for the next few days will be to familiarise myself with the building and identify the mouse hotspots but please do say 'hello' to me if I'm in your area.
>
> I'm also keen to meet my fellow four-pawed member of staff,

Rocco, who I understand visits the first floor quite a lot. He recently won the People's Choice Award at the Westminster Dog Show so I'm certainly in distinguished company. I also need to pop next door for a meeting with Larry. Don't believe what you read on social media, there's no competition here and he's already sent me a welcome present. I'm sure the two of us will make a formidable duo to rid the corridors of Whitehall from rodents.

There is no doubt Palmerston caused a stir and proved very popular, with a sale of buns and cakes at the Foreign Office helping raise the funds required to help him make his home in McDonald's office. He soon had his own line of 'merch'.

'When he arrived, we had this line in Palmerston mugs and reusable coffee cups and that generated a certain amount of money, which paid for his food and also his insurance. So Palmerston was entirely self-financed,' says McDonald.

But one branch of McDonald's empire – or, perhaps more accurately, Palmerston's new empire – was initially unconvinced of the power of the feline: the press office. McDonald recalls that

the comms people at the beginning were super sniffy, you know; they thought this was frivolous and a waste of time. 'Why were we even bothering?' But then they did agree that he should have a social media presence, and we got the @diplomog handle on Twitter. And of course, as soon as he arrived, the comms people saw he was a success. And if you want to make the Foreign Office seem a little less scary, a little bit more relatable, having an office cat helps that.

In fairness to the communications staff at the Foreign Office, they did lean into Palmerston's arrival by sending out the following comments to journalists:

> Palmerston is HM Diplomatic Service's newest arrival and, in the role of FCO Chief Mouser, will assist our pest controllers in keeping down the number of mice in our King Charles Street building.
>
> Palmerston's domestic posting will have zero cost to the public purrse as a staff kitty will be used to pay for him and all aspects of his welfur.
>
> We have worked closely with Battersea Dogs & Cats Home on Palmerston's deployment and they have inspected his new home, as they do for all pawtential new owners of their rescue cats.

Palmerston's profile grew quickly. While less popular as a medium now, McDonald says that when Palmerston arrived

> all diplomats were on Twitter; all were trying to build their followers. So nearly every foreign ambassador who came into my office asked about Palmerston and wanted a photo with Palmerston to put on Twitter.
>
> Palmerston rapidly gained Twitter followers in the tens of thousands. The Foreign Secretary at the time was Philip Hammond, and he joked that within three months, Palmerston would have more followers than him!

Palmerston has, in fact, never quite overtaken Lord Hammond, who has 102,800 followers on Twitter at the time of writing; Palmerston is within a paw's swiping distance at 101,400 followers.

Palmerston settled in well initially, with his first mouse kill reported within a fortnight or so. The Foreign Office said in March 2018 that Palmerston's reported catches since the start of 2017 were thirty-eight hits, but 'figures are likely to be much higher, as these are only reported sightings'.

Palmerston is also immortalised in the parliamentary record, Hansard. In May 2016, a month after Palmerston arrived at the Foreign Office, Hammond was quizzed by Conservative MP Keith Simpson on this departmental feline's credentials and whether Palmerston had 'been positively vetted by the security service and scanned for bugs by GCHQ?' At the height of the Brexit debate, Simpson asked, 'Can you assure the House, and the more paranoid element of the Brexiteers, of Palmerston's British provenance and that he is not a long-term mole working for the EU Commission?' Hammond replied:

> He is definitely not a mole, and I can categorically assure you that Palmerston has been regularly vetted. As for being a sleeper, he is definitely a sleeper, I am told very often in my office. His attendance record has been 100 per cent. My experts tell me that pretty much rules out the possibility of him being a Commission employee.

Palmerston quickly became a well-known and popular character in and around Westminster. However, despite receiving a gift from Larry on his arrival, the two would not always enjoy a positive relationship. The Foreign Office – Palmerston's territory

– backs directly on to Downing Street – Larry's domain. Cat fights ensued, some of which were caught in dramatic images, not least by Justin Ng, a photographer who has chronicled both cats with his lens during long days waiting for politicians to appear on Downing Street. Ng is a big cat person; he got to know Palmerston well while he was at the Foreign Office and is still great mates with Larry. Which, at least at first, was more than could be said for Palmerston. 'Initially, the two of them just never got on,' Ng tells *Political Animals*. 'It was Larry's territory, and Palmerston was invading it. But towards the end of their time, I felt like they had a kind of respect for one another. They would, quite often in the summer, sleep near each other. There was at least half a metre's distance between them. But they would sleep near each other as if they were begrudging friends.'

Analysing those initial fights and their later truce, cat behaviourist and author of *Being Your Cat* Celia Haddon says:

> Some cats don't understand when they are beaten. They keep fighting back even if they are going to lose each fight. If Palmerston's wounds were on his head and chest or, on one occasion, his ear, it shows he was facing up to Larry.
>
> If they were on the base of his tail or backside, then he may have had to flee. No wonder he got rather stressed. Repeated fights are stressful for both the winner and the loser, but worse for the loser. In footage of the fights, it looks as if Larry was taking the initiative in the fighting – which of course was because Palmerston was moving into his territory.

'The journalists on Downing Street love this because they're there staked out hour after hour, come rain, come shine,' says McDonald. 'It's only interesting around the famous black door from time to time. So this feud between the two cats at Downing Street provided entertainment for many photojournalists over several years.'

'Palmerston is the more aggressive cat,' says Ng. Palmerston's bloodiest encounter with prey came in July 2018. 'He did actually kill a duckling. A duck with three of her brood was walking towards the pond in St James's Park, towards the side of Downing Street. Palmerston noticed so he grabbed one of them. Someone actually got a photo of that and it made the news. Bloodbath. Grim stuff.'

When not killing his own food, Palmerston, who is a hefty cat, was not averse to nicking treats that weren't his. For Larry, on at least one occasion, it was a case of 'you snooze, you lose'. Ng recalls the time a police officer brought Dreamies for Larry and shook them in his direction. Larry remained asleep, but Palmerston 'slowly snuck down towards the police officer to get Larry's Dreamies. Larry was completely unaware of what was going on.'

As is sometimes the case with government ministers, the cats of Westminster occasionally exceed their brief; Palmerston certainly carried on that ministerial tradition when it came to food. It wasn't just Larry's supper that he snaffled – Palmerston was thrown out of No. 10 on a few occasions for attempting and occasionally succeeding at that one. A little further down Whitehall in the Cabinet Office, Evie and Ossie prowl the corridors and their grub proved to be an irresistible temptation.

Evie is black and white and to some degree looks like a smaller version of Palmerston. 'We caught Palmerston in there one day eating her food,' recalls Sue Gray, who worked as director of propriety and ethics at the Cabinet Office but, at least as importantly, was cat mum to Evie and Ossie (see Chapter Seven). 'The staff thought it was Evie, but, I mean, Palmerston was about ten times the size! He'd snuck in through the back door from the Foreign Office, just walked up the stairs and there he was eating away at their food.'

As many cat owners know, this cheekiness by Palmerston is repeated by cats the world over. 'Nicking other cats' food is natural behaviour,' says Haddon.

> Many cats like variety, which is why cat food comes in different flavours. So stolen food can be preferable, just for the change. If Palmerston is a bit of a foodie, keen on grub, then naturally he would want to sample other cats' food. And as a stray before Battersea rescued him, he would have known hunger. Food is usually more important to cats that have experienced hunger.

But, as McDonald notes, it was Palmerston's love of food – and his popularity with civil servants – that led to problems for the moggy.

> He was a nice cat and that was, in the end, one of the problems. There are between two and three thousand people on any given day in the building and they would come across Palmerston and pet him like he was their own – not only stroke him but feed him Dreamies. Think of this in human terms: feeding Palmerston Dreamies is like force-feeding a

human Mars bars. And so he put on weight. He began to get a bit stressed by the attention as well. So we consulted a vet.

Sonia Khan was a civil servant at the Department for International Trade, which was based in the Foreign Office building, and got to know Palmerston while she worked there. 'He was a funny one,' remembers Khan.

> Palmerston was actually the opposite of all the other cats of Whitehall in that he was quite happy to come up and get a lot of comfort.
>
> But I remember at one point he had too much to eat, because a memo went round asking people to stop feeding him. I think he was starting to become very, very overweight. You couldn't walk two minutes in the building without finding someone who had a pot of Dreamies or other snacks ready for him, because he was such a curious and friendly and engaging cat and always wanted to know what people were doing.

A different cat in temperament, certainly, from Larry at No. 10 and Gladstone in the Treasury. 'The key to Larry is that he is of a phlegmatic disposition; he strikes me as very unfazed,' says McDonald.

> But the other Whitehall cats, at some point, all became quite stressed by the attention they were getting and that was certainly the case with Palmerston – he started plucking his own fur, so bald patches appeared on his paws. He just needed to take a step back. And it did him the power of good.

Palmerston took a six-month holiday at the home of one of McDonald's private secretaries, which provided a much-needed break from the constant petting – and from the Dreamies. The private secretary lived in a flat, so Palmerston perhaps didn't shift all the pounds he needed to, but he returned to the Foreign Office in rude health, happy and full of energy. To keep his snacking and stress under control, new guidelines were introduced: the Palmerston Protocols, a series of rules to make sure Palmerston's stomping ground was limited so that he wasn't wandering too much and, crucially, was not being fed too many treats by good-natured staff.

Despite these efforts, it was soon clear that the Foreign Office was not where Palmerston would be happiest and that it was time for him to move on a more permanent basis.

McDonald recalls, 'Palmerston's longer break in 2020 coincided with coronavirus, with my private secretary who lived on the edge of the South Downs National Park. But when I told folk he'd "gone to the countryside" they thought it was shorthand for, well, you know…'

Palmerston loved his new life in the South Downs. Ever the media-savvy cat, he announced his retirement in a letter to McDonald sent on 7 August 2020, on the eve of International Cat Day.

Dear Simon,

After four years serving as the Foreign and Commonwealth Office's Chief Mouser, I believe the time has come for me go into retirement so I can spend more time relaxing away from the limelight.

The spread of coronavirus around the world has caused many, like me, to begin working from home. I assure you that I have been as diligent as ever. While I have not been able to catch the King Charles Street mice from afar, my diplomatic efforts on engaging the mouse species have seen a significant uptick. I have pawed numerous memorandums and been on the winning side of many hard-fought negotiations. My diplomatic craft has had positive results.

I have found life away from the front line more relaxed, quieter, and easier. I have enjoyed climbing trees and patrolling the fields around my new home in the countryside. The family in my new home have also been pleasingly assiduous in providing for my every need. Of course I loved the hustle and bustle of the office. I will miss hearing the footsteps of an ambassador and sprinting to my hideout to see who it is. My signature move: pretending to be asleep while overhearing all the foreign dignitaries' conversations, will be a major loss for our intelligence gathering. But as I grow older, I must take a step back from diplomatic duties and enjoy some me-time.

I have been delighted to meet representatives from all over the world and I hope that I have done you proud in putting the UK's best foot, or paw, forward in each interaction. My 105,000 Twitter followers show that even those with four legs and fur have an important part to play in the UK's global effort. I have championed our work, built our relationships, and celebrated the diversity of our staff. I have also set up my own parallel network: our diplocats and diplodogs have been excellent ambassadors who, I have faith, will continue their exemplary efforts without me.

Although I am ending my formal role here, I will always be an ambassador for the UK and the new Foreign, Commonwealth and Development Office.

Yours,

Palmerston

Responding to this turn of events, a spokesman for Battersea said:

As one of our most illustrious former residents, Palmerston has been a fantastic ambassador for Battersea. During his tenure as Chief Mouser at the Foreign Office, he has perfectly demonstrated how incredible rescue cats are, as well as the joy that they can bring to people when given a second chance.

We have loved following his prolific career over the past four years and we look forward to hearing about his future adventures, as he swaps international diplomacy for a life of leisure. On behalf of all the staff, cats and even the dogs, at Battersea, we wish Palmerston all the very best with this next chapter of his nine lives.

'The thing about cats is they choose their people,' says McDonald. 'You know, dogs are much more willing to be guided. But Palmerston, when he got to the Hampshire countryside, completely connected with the husband of my private secretary, a man called Andy Murdoch. So Andy became his person.'

Murdoch, a diplomat and former officer in the Royal Navy, took up the post of governor of Bermuda in January 2025 and brought Palmerston with him. Followers of Palmerston's

@diplomog Twitter account were captivated by his update on 27 December 2024: 'I've got my Dreamies packed, my fur is purr-fect, and I'm ready for an adventure. Stay tuned for some exciting news.' Just over a month later, on 4 February 2025, Palmerston confirmed that he had arrived in Bermuda. 'Diplomacy and a purr-fect role have lured me out of retirement,' he announced. 'I've just started work as feline relations consultant (semi-retired) to the new governor of Bermuda. I've been busy meeting very welcoming Bermudians.' Bermuda's daily newspaper, the *Royal Gazette*, reported that Palmerston was 'attending only the meetings he deems important, offering advice when necessary and, of course, indulging in well-earned naps'. Palmerston later revealed that the international pet transport company Fetchapet and its employee Sally were responsible for his 3,500-mile trip west to the British Overseas Territory.

'Palmerston will love the climate in Bermuda,' says Haddon.

Cats enjoy heat. Sometimes they are called 'heat-seeking puss-iles'. After all, the domestic cat started life as a Libyan wildcat that moved into human settlements in the fertile crescent where it is a great deal hotter than the UK. There will be house mice in Bermuda for him. And as cats eat a lot of lizards in hotter climates, I expect he has become a keen lizard hunter too. An added bonus is that an ambassador's private residence is quieter than a busy office.

Back in England, McDonald could finally prove to his doubters that Palmerston was alive and well. The same day Palmerston announced his reappearance in Bermuda, McDonald tweeted:

'Most frequent question I field since leaving @FCDOGovUK is: "Whatever happened to Palmerston?" The answer – retirement to countryside – usually treated as euphemism for "He died." Now we have proof of life in Bermuda! Enjoy your latest assignment @DiploMog!'

'It's just a nice wee story,' says McDonald. 'The governor's garden is apparently thirty acres. I do fear for the bird life.'

Rehoming and welfare manager at Battersea's London cattery, Bridie Williams, said at the time:

> Everyone at Battersea wishes Palmerston the very best in his new post as feline relations consultant, working in his special role as the Foreign Office's first feline diplomat. As one of Battersea's most notable former residents, Palmerston has helped shine a light on the joy that rescue cats can bring to people's lives and we look forward to hearing more about his new adventures in due course.

Enoch Powell once said all political careers end in failure, but it would appear that this is not the case for Palmerston, who is now a star not just in the United Kingdom but in Bermuda and around the world. He's even inspired other British embassies to adopt their own cats, such as those in Mongolia and Jordan. The latter appointed its chief mouser in 2017; Lawrence of Abdoun was described by Reuters as 'a fluffy black-and-white tom who, according to his Twitter feed, reports directly to the Foreign Office's Palmerston'. Lawrence was of course named after T. E. Lawrence, also known as Lawrence of Arabia, the British army officer who fought against the Ottoman Empire during the First

World War. The deputy ambassador to Jordan, Laura Dauban, said of the diplocat, 'Apart from his mousing duties, he reaches out to followers on Twitter. What's quite interesting is the British public are seeing the UK embassy in Jordan in a different light.'

However, even Lawrence was not immune to social media trolls. 'He's been a bit upset because some people have said he looked a bit fat in the last tweet he did, so he'll be doing some exercises and posting to sort of rectify that situation,' Dauban told Reuters.

Despite this unpleasantness towards Lawrence, who is apparently thriving despite not having tweeted in a personal capacity since 2020, Palmerston's global influence is apparent for all to see, inspiring other cats around the world. 'Larry is a sort of superstar,' says McDonald. 'The Angelina Jolie of the Whitehall feline world – but Palmerston would definitely be best supporting actor.'

CHAPTER SEVEN

EVIE AND OSSIE AT THE CABINET OFFICE

Mother-and-son duo Evie and Ossie patrol the corridors of the Cabinet Office, the central nervous system of government. This is where the boss of the whole civil service has his empire. That boss is sadly not a cat but a human being: Sir Chris Wormald. He's also the Cabinet Secretary, sitting beside the Prime Minister at Cabinet next door in 10 Downing Street and guiding him through the process of governing. But when Evie and Ossie arrived in November 2016, it was Sir (later Lord) Jeremy Heywood who ran the show.

The slight issue was that Heywood was no fan of cats. Indeed, his antipathy was such that, on one occasion, he sent an email to his chief of staff, Kata Escott, outlining his displeasure with a particular habit of Evie and Ossie's. Escott then forwarded the email to the cats' biggest fan – and, as she had brought them into the building, their effective 'mum' – senior civil servant Sue Gray, who would later become Sir Keir Starmer's chief of staff. The subject line was 'Cat Faeces' and it was written in a style Gray remembers as being 'the classic civil servant… while obviously not being happy!'

Heywood wrote: 'Can I just say that I have had enough of walking past CF on the staircase? This is a place of work, not a zoo or pet shop. Final warning.'

'It was a very Jeremy email,' Gray tells *Political Animals*. 'So I messaged him back to say, who's the final warning for – me or the cats? He couldn't stand them. And yet, he kept his room really hot, it was like a sauna, so they would gravitate to his office, lie on his desk and he was really not happy.' Suzanne Heywood, Jeremy's wife and the author of his biography, *What Does Jeremy Think?*, mentioned the email in her eulogy at his funeral in 2018. 'We were all in stitches,' chuckled Gray, remembering her former boss with affection.

Suzanne Heywood confirmed to *Political Animals* that cats, along with 'karaoke, helicopters, rats and urban foxes', were amongst the things her husband most detested. However, she emphasised that Evie and Ossie were still well looked after; they loved sitting on the comfy chair in her husband's office when he wasn't around, and his private office staff kept Dreamies ready for them alongside the rest of the office snacks on their treat table.

'Occasionally we had people that have worked in the Cabinet Office who have an allergy, so we took steps to make sure to keep the cats contained in a particular area – that's done in consultation with the individual,' remembers Gray. 'I don't think there was ever a problem with any individual, apart from, I think, Jeremy, who was the person who really loathed them.' However, plenty of other people loved them.

Many of the Whitehall cats' names – though Larry is an exception – have a strong association with the history of the building they live in. Evie is named after Dame Evelyn Sharp, the first female Permanent Secretary, while Ossie is named after Sir Edward Osmotherly, author of the Osmotherly Rules, which set out how civil servants should give evidence to select committees.

Evie and Ossie are rescue cats from the Celia Hammond Animal Trust. They were found as strays living on the streets of east London. Evie, the mother, arrived at the rescue centre with three kittens, of whom Ossie was one. She was nervous in the beginning, but soon became a very friendly, calm and sweet-natured cat. Two of the kittens were rehomed together, but the trust wanted Evie to stay with at least one of her kittens. 'At the Celia Hammond Trust, we continue to rescue and rehome unwanted and abandoned cats in these very challenging times,' the charity's founder, Celia Hammond, tells *Political Animals*. 'There is the huge pressure of large numbers of unwanted pets post-pandemic and in the cost-of-living crisis. We are always grateful for support of our charity, whether that is from members of the public adopting animals or, in this case, perhaps a more high-profile rehoming!'

Evie is very petite, black and white and long-haired, and Ossie is a larger boy, pure black and short-haired. Gray says:

> They are indoor cats, although Evie occasionally has frightened the life out of us by going for a little walk through Treasury passage and out into Horse Guards. And because she's so slim and tiny, she's able to sneak under the gate, whereas Ossie would never have any chance of sneaking under the gate – he'd get stuck!

Occasionally Evie's escapes have involved Gray and others heading to neighbouring government departments:

> I actually had to go one evening to the Scotland Office in

Dover House because Evie was in their garden, and I asked if I could go through the back door to get her out, rescue her. Then there'd be me, a couple of other people in the Cabinet Office, the Scotland Office, and we're all trying to catch Evie and bring her back. And she, of course, doesn't like being picked up. But Ossie's favourite thing is being groomed. He loves people brushing him. He's an attention seeker.

One of the main places Ossie seeks – and receives – the attention he craves is in one of the main corridors of the Cabinet Office, dating back to Tudor times. There sits a glass case housing a model of the old Palace of Whitehall, the top of which has become a favourite relaxation spot for both cats, although the petite Evie is perhaps more safely accommodated than the chonky Ossie. 'Evie does sit on it sometimes, she's quite petite,' says Gray. 'But Ossie fully stretches out, taking up the whole thing. It's surprising it hasn't collapsed on the model! He just loves lying on it, and then he watches everybody going past and expects to be stroked.'

The Cabinet Office is right next door to No. 10 and numerous staff pass between the buildings every day via a link corridor. Therefore, many senior civil servants, including Gray, were very aware of Larry and saw him on a frequent basis. But they were not No. 10 copycats in adopting Evie and Ossie; rather, it was their own rodent problem that inspired the Cabinet Office to get its own cats. Gray recalls how 'you could be sitting at your desk and a mouse would run past your feet in meetings'.

Unlike some of the Whitehall cats, Gray says, Evie and Ossie stay where they are meant to be – usually.

Occasionally, Evie and Ossie will walk to the link door with No. 10 and they might look through, but they aren't allowed in. Ossie in particular is very happy for the doors to open and to jump in. Evie will just look. I'm not sure what would happen if Ossie met Larry. Oh, goodness!

After a clean bill of health for the building from the Celia Hammond Animal Trust inspectors, the Cabinet Office was deemed a proper home for the cats. With the all-clear from the trust, Gray, who was then head of propriety and ethics for the civil service, dispatched one of her staff, a senior civil servant called Eirian Walsh Atkins, to the Hammond shelter to choose a cat. But a cat quickly turned into two cats, as they didn't want to separate mother and son. Hammond tells *Political Animals*:

> I remember the unusual home visit of the Cabinet Office well. As is the case with all our adoptions, we as a charity visit and carry out a home check first, to ensure the animals will be cared for well and they will be happy. My concern initially was that the cats would get lost within the rabbit warren of the Cabinet Office and wouldn't be able to find their way around such a big building. The cats were started off in one big carpeted room and were then allowed to explore further around the building. Fortunately, this was successful and the cats settled in well.

Evie likes to spend much of her time on the fourth floor of the Cabinet Office near Gray's old office, in an informal area where civil servants can have meetings, separated by cloth-covered screens for privacy. 'Evie sits at the top of the screen,' says Gray, 'even sleeping on it. And if things get too noisy, she'll make her displeasure known by jumping down and frightening the life out of people who didn't even realise that she was sitting up there.'

Another favourite perch for Evie is the red velvet throne in the old Cabinet Room in the Cabinet Office, but, as Gray explains, often the cat leaves too much of herself behind. 'You have to take the Sellotape out quite a lot, and the brush, to lift up the hairs. She loves sitting on that throne!' says Gray.

One issue with the Cabinet Office buildings is that during the week things are very busy and the cats get lots of attention, whereas at the weekends – and during the pandemic lockdowns – they tend to be very quiet. But the cats often find where the action is, particularly if COBRA, the government's emergency committee, has to meet to deal with a rapidly developing situation. 'Ossie is so outgoing,' says Gray.

> So, at weekends, if there's a COBRA or there are people in, he will find them. Both of them are a great calming influence, but Ossie is particularly so. If there's been a difficult meeting, people come out and there he is. They stroke him. And I think it's a really amazing calmness. It's the same with staff. He'll wander around and sit on their desks.

But all is not always calm between the two cats. Mother and son rarely encounter one another these days, but when they do, they have been known to come to blows. 'Every now and again, she has to tell him off, and she does,' says Gray.

Atkins, who first picked them up from the trust, is still Evie and Ossie's main carer, with security staff at the Cabinet Office

ABOVE Laddie Boy, President Warren Harding's Airedale terrier, celebrating his birthday with a dog-biscuit cake. The first true celebrity White House pet, Laddie Boy was interviewed by the *Washington Star* and 'authored' a number of letters and articles published in papers such as the *New York Times*. He had his own seat in Cabinet meetings attended by the President.
© Herbert E. French/Library of Congress

LEFT President Franklin D. Roosevelt drives around Hyde Park, New York, accompanied by Fala, his Scottish terrier. Another celebrity, Fala appeared in newsreels and even in an Oscar-winning film, *Princess O'Rourke*. Fala is the only White House pet to have been immortalised in a President's memorial statue in Washington DC.
© Library of Congress

BELOW LEFT President John F. Kennedy's daughter Caroline riding her horse Macaroni, led by Secret Service agent Bob Foster. Macaroni was one of a number of animals given to the Kennedys. Others included a dog, Pushinka, from Soviet Union leader Nikita Khrushchev; Sardar, a bay gelding from the President of Pakistan; and two deer and a pony named Leprechaun from Irish President Éamon de Valera.
© Robert Knudsen/White House Photographs/John F. Kennedy Presidential Library and Museum, Boston

Winston Churchill feeds his albino kangaroo, Digger, at London Zoo in 1947. It has widely been forgotten that Churchill was a huge lover of animals – not only domestic pets such as the cats and dogs who accompanied him to meetings and dinners but also far more exotic animals. As well as Digger, he had another kangaroo named Matilda, a leopard named Sheba and a lion called Rota, all of whom he donated to the zoo.

© Bettman/Corbis Historical via Getty Images

President Lyndon B. Johnson outraged animal rights activists in May 1964 by lifting his dog Him by the ears. 'It does them good to let them yelp,' he claimed. Johnson had two other dogs while in office, Her and Yuki.

© Cecil Stoughton/Lyndon Baines Johnson Presidential Library

Bill and Hillary Clinton's cat, Socks, at the White House briefing podium in 1993. Socks jumped into their daughter Chelsea's arms when she was at a piano lesson in 1991 and thereafter became part of the family – despite Bill Clinton being allergic to cats. While in office, the Clintons adopted Buddy, a chocolate Labrador retriever, but he and Socks never got on. © William J. Clinton Presidential Library

President Vladimir Putin of Russia has frequently used photos of him bare-chested on horses as a mechanism to emphasise his machismo. He also deliberately brought his Labrador Koni to a meeting with former German Chancellor Angela Merkel to intimidate her, knowing she has a fear of dogs. © Alexey Druzhinin/AFP via Getty Images

ABOVE LEFT This photocall was organised by communications supremo Alastair Campbell to help combat the rumours circulating that Tony Blair's wife Cherie was trying to get rid of Humphrey the cat. She did let slip that she was no fan of the animal, but there were other reasons for Humphrey's exit from Downing Street in 1997. Tony Blair later described the whole affair as the biggest scandal of his first year in office. Let's face it, from this photo alone, we can tell that Humphrey knew the score.
© PA Images/Alamy Stock Photo

ABOVE RIGHT President George W. Bush's Scottish terrier Barney examines presents under the White House Christmas tree in 2005. Barney was most well known for his six *Barney Cam* videos, which gave a 'dog's-eye view' of the White House and featured celebrity guests such as Michael Phelps, Tony Blair and Dolly Parton. The Bushes had two other pets: Miss Beazley, another Scottie, and India, a black American shorthair cat.
© George W. Bush Presidential Library and Museum/NARA

President Barack Obama and Bo in the Oval Office. Bo was a Portuguese water dog, a hypoallergenic breed chosen because Obama's eldest daughter Malia is allergic to some dogs. Bo joined the family shortly after they moved into the White House and was trained as a comfort animal.
© The Office of Barack and Michelle Obama

Liberal Democrat MP Steve Darling, who represents Torbay, with Jennie his guide dog. Jennie has become a celebrity in her own right and was once admonished by the Liberal Democrat Chief Whip for 'crossing the floor'. In reality, she had just nipped over to the Labour benches to see a friend.

David Cameron with Larry the cat in Downing Street on his last day as Prime Minister. Larry came to Downing Street eight months into Cameron's premiership; however, it was rumoured that there was tension between them. Cameron addressed these unfounded tales in his final Prime Minister's Questions, showing the Commons a photograph of Larry sat on his lap and declaring, 'I do [love him], and I have photographic evidence to prove it.' The photograph shown here was taken on the same day but has never been published. It offers a warm, light-hearted window into Cameron and Larry's relationship.
Courtesy of Lord Cameron

Evie, named after Dame Evelyn Sharp, lives at the Cabinet Office and helps with their rodent problem. She was found as a stray with three kittens in east London. Two were relocated together, but the Celia Hammond Trust insisted that Evie stay with one of her kittens – her son, Ossie. Evie likes to sit on the throne in the old Cabinet room and is known for her occasional escapades into neighbouring government departments.
Courtesy of Baroness Gray

Ossie, Evie's son, keeping a restricted document safe on the Cabinet Secretary's desk. He loves attention and can often be found lounging atop a glass case housing a model of the old Palace of Whitehall. Many civil servants find comfort and calm in petting him or his mum in times of stress.
Courtesy of Emma Southard

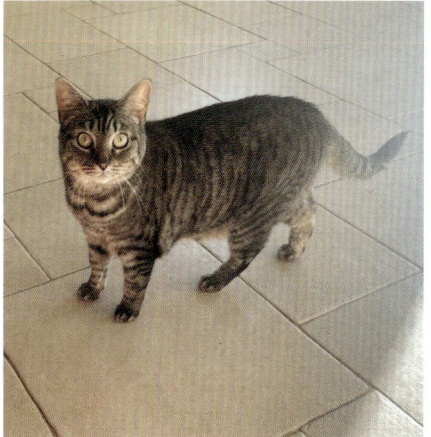

Susie Gray, named after former senior civil servant and No. 10 chief of staff Sue Gray. Baroness Gray led the Partygate report investigating gatherings held in Downing Street during the Covid lockdowns. Shortly afterwards, Mayhew, an animal welfare charity, got in touch to let her office know they'd named a rescue cat after her and the baroness promptly adopted her namesake.
Courtesy of Baroness Gray

ABOVE Former special adviser Liz Sugg (*left*) introduces Larry the cat to President Barack Obama at No. 10 while Prime Minister David Cameron looks on, May 2011. Larry is someone that many Downing Street visitors want to meet – from US Presidents to One Direction band members.
© Pete Souza/Official White House Photo

LEFT Chief mouser Larry keeps a watchful eye at the famous black door of 10 Downing Street. He has been in post at the Cabinet Office since 2011 and has been photographed thousands of times, becoming one of the most enduring symbols of Downing Street. These days, he is renowned for his phlegmatic disposition, though he has been known to come to blows with other cats and political animals. As an older gent, Larry's territory is respected and new feline arrivals (most recently Jojo and Prince, the Starmers' cats) are kept away from him.
Courtesy of Horatio Lovering

LEFT Larry fights with Chancellor George Osborne's cat Freya in Downing Street, October 2012. The two shared the job of mousing No. 10 and No. 11, but they often butted heads. Freya was known for exploring the local area, including Westminster's favoured pub, the Red Lion. She was rehomed with one of the Downing Street butlers after she had a nasty run-in with a car.
Courtesy of Steve Back

Palmerston and Sir Simon McDonald catch up on the Permanent Secretary's floor at the Foreign Office. McDonald brought in Palmerston in 2016 to deal with the Foreign Office's mouse problem and Palmerston was very good at his job. He and Larry fought at first, but eventually they grew to have a healthy respect for each other. He is a very friendly cat but got quite stressed from receiving so much attention, so he retired in 2020.

Courtesy of Lord McDonald

Palmerston working as feline relations consultant with his new cat dad, Andy Murdoch, governor of Bermuda. Palmerston's quieter life suits him much better and he has inspired other British embassies to adopt their own cats.

© Foreign, Commonwealth and Development Office Twitter

Prime Minister Boris Johnson takes Dilyn to his local polling station to vote in the local elections, May 2022. Dilyn, who has a misaligned jaw, was adopted by Johnson and his then partner (now wife) Carrie Symonds from a shelter. Well known for his boisterous behaviour, Dilyn also became famous as the focal point of a falling out between Symonds and Dominic Cummings, Johnson's chief adviser.

Courtesy of Justin Ng

ABOVE LEFT The author Peter Cardwell, then working as a special adviser with the Northern Ireland Office, with Gladstone the Treasury cat in 2018. Gladstone was an effective mouser but tended to keep to himself. He found the constant hustle and bustle too stressful and retired in 2019 to live with one of the civil servants he used to work alongside.

ABOVE RIGHT Rishi Sunak, as Chancellor, prepares for the 2021 Budget alongside Nova the fox red Labrador retriever. Nova lived in Downing Street for four years and frequently attended receptions. Walking his dog helped Sunak to relax, get some exercise and temporarily step away from the busy pace of life of being Chancellor and, later, Prime Minister. Courtesy of Rishi Sunak

Prime Minister Sir Keir Starmer works in his office accompanied by Prince the kitten. Prince joined the Starmers' other cat Jojo shortly after the family moved into No. 10. The two get on well, although they are deliberately kept well clear of Larry's territory. © Simon Dawson/No. 10 Downing Street

feeding the cats at weekends. During Gray's tenure, she paid for the food out of her own pocket, but since she left there have been sales of merchandise, including mugs bearing the cats' images, at the Cabinet Office to raise funds.

The generosity and love that Cabinet Office civil servants have for the cats was exhibited in 2022 when Ossie had a close shave with his health after licking some lily leaves and eating part of the plant. As many cat owners know, lilies are highly toxic to cats and can lead to kidney damage and even death. Ossie was rushed to an animal hospital, where he was given fluids and charcoal treatment. Thankfully, Ossie's vet gave the moggy a 'good chance of success'. Nadhim Zahawi, then a senior Cabinet Office minister holding the title of Chancellor of the Duchy of Lancaster, shared a photo of Ossie online and made clear he had been allowed home. Zahawi posted: 'Very pleased to report that Ossie is now back in the Cabinet Office having had treatment and is on the road to recovery!' While Ossie was away, his mum Evie was found sitting near a picture of her son, perhaps sensing his absence. But the vet bill for Ossie's treatment was around £1,000. Again, the civil servants who love Ossie so much clubbed together to raise the money, after one of Ossie's human friends put up posters around the Cabinet Office.

Thankfully, Ossie made a full recovery and was soon back on pawtrol at the Cabinet Office, being fussed over not just by civil servants but by the politicians who use the offices too. One such politician, Sir Oliver Dowden, who served as Deputy Prime Minister under Rishi Sunak, was a particular fan of Evie and Ossie.

The opposition is entitled to various briefings about national security issues, and these are often held at the Cabinet Office.

Gray, who by this stage had left the civil service and was working as Sir Keir Starmer's chief of staff, remembers one memorable national security briefing given to the opposition that was led by Dowden.

> I was coming in for a briefing. And Oliver started the meeting by talking to me about the cats, just updating me on how they were and how he was looking after them. And I was with Keir and [then shadow Foreign Secretary] David Lammy and I could see them just thinking, 'What on earth is going on here?'

Gray had cemented her status as chief cat mum of Whitehall a couple of years earlier. She had spent months looking into gatherings held in government buildings – including in No. 10 – that broke lockdown rules and she was all over the news as the report's author. A moment of light relief came on 26 May 2022, the day after the Partygate report was released, when Mayhew Animal Home in north-west London contacted Gray's office to tell her staff a grey cat had been brought in and had been given the name of Susie Gray. Very quickly, a home for rescue cat Susie Gray was secured – with her namesake!

> I got this message, and I straight away discussed it with the civil service team. I said, 'I'm going to take this cat. We'll bring it in here.' I went back to the team at the rescue home and I said, 'You know, I'll have that cat,' thinking I'd bring it into the Cabinet Office. And then they said to me, 'It's got a sibling that

it's really attached to.' And I said, 'I'll have that one as well.' I still thought I'd bring both of them in. And then I decided that was quite difficult, because we already had two cats. So I have got these two cats at my home.

They're grey: one has grey stripes and a white tummy, and the other one's just completely grey, stripy. They are so alike and they love each other. Brother and sister. They sleep together. They argue a little bit; they play.

Lisa Guiney, head of operations at Mayhew, told *Political Animals*:

> We sometimes name animals who come into our rescue home after celebrities and people in the headlines. In May 2022, Sue Gray's Partygate report was all over the news and at the same time we had a little grey cat and her brother come to us. A foster carer nicknamed the girl kitten Susie Gray – we thought it might be fun to let the actual Sue Gray know, so we contacted her office. What a brilliant surprise when Sue herself decided to adopt Susie!
>
> It sounds as though Susie and her brother are thriving in their home, which is what every cat and dog deserve.
>
> At Mayhew we believe that every animal that comes through our doors is worthy of a second chance and a loving home, and we're so pleased that Sue Gray has given exactly that to these two lovely cats.

Gray is now a member of the House of Lords, Baroness Gray of Tottenham, but her former colleagues at the Cabinet Office still keep her updated on the adventures of Evie and Ossie. Susie Gray and her brother remain happily at Baroness Gray's home and are loved and cared for by a true cat person.

CHAPTER EIGHT

GLADSTONE AT THE TREASURY

The Treasury building, just down Whitehall from the Foreign Office and Downing Street, houses a number of government departments and offices, including the Northern Ireland Office, where I worked as a special adviser for about a year and a half.

Making myself a cup of tea one day just yards from my desk, I saw a civil servant with an animal carrier. I asked her who was inside and she told me – to my great delight – that it was Gladstone, the Treasury cat, on his way to a routine check-up at the vet's. She mentioned that Gladstone's 'office' was only two floors up from my own and that I was welcome to pop in. I soon became a semi-regular visitor, giving Gladstone a little stroke as I put a few quid into his little ceramic money box – a cat-shaped one, naturally – which was a small contribution to his food, vet bills and upkeep costs. When I saw Gladstone, he seemed so happy and well looked after.

Gladstone was known as the best mouser in government. Treasury civil servants were very proud of his record and were even offered the chance to buy mugs and Christmas cards with his photo on them. I bought one of the mugs myself. On hearing its price was an eye-watering £7.50, a senior civil servant at the Northern Ireland Office, who had previously worked alongside Gladstone's colleagues, raised his eyes to the ceiling and exclaimed, 'Classic Treasury!'

Gladstone was born in December 2014 and, like Palmerston at the Foreign Office and Larry at No. 10, was a rescue cat from Battersea Dogs & Cats Home, who had taken him in after he was found homeless in central London, hungry and without a microchip. At around eighteen months old, he came to the Treasury to take up the position of chief mouser. Originally called Timmy, he was renamed after former Prime Minister William Ewart Gladstone, who had served as Chancellor no fewer than four times – more than any other person to date. Sir John Kingman, who was Second Permanent Secretary at the Treasury at the time, decided to bring Gladstone on board. The announcement was made on 29 July 2016, although Gladstone had been in situ for a few months before his presence was made public. Like his com-cat-riots across Whitehall, Gladstone did not cost the taxpayer a penny.

Gladstone's arrival made the front page of the *Evening Standard*. He was pictured beside the Chancellor's ministerial red box and with the headline 'Catfight: Meet Gladstone, the new puss in Whitehall'.

His first Instagram post read:

Hello! I'm Gladstone, a charming eighteen-month-old domestic short hair (which makes me a moggie). I recently moved into my new home at Her Majesty's Treasury, where I'll be tackling their mouse problem. The civil servants who work there adopted me from @batterseadogsandcatshome, and I've been settling into public service life for a couple of weeks #publicservice #purrsstrings.

Soon, his Instagram was full of Gladstone in colourful bow ties, videos of him being brushed, inspecting his fan mail and playing with toys sent by well-wishers. Other gifts included Christmas baubles from Brazil, a personalised collar and a Halloween knitted scarf from Australia.

Photos on his social media included the cat on a little red lead as he was being walked around the Treasury building in his early days there, before he was allowed to wander more independently.

His handlers played up to media coverage of feline territorial battles between the Foreign Office cat, Palmerston, and Larry in Downing Street (see Chapter Eleven). 'Gladstone' captioned a photo of him being transported in a cat carrier: 'Me on my first day at my new home. The humans had to keep me in this cage in case I ran down the street and tormented some other mouser called "Larry". Personally, I have never heard of him.'

In September 2018, *The Sun* reported that there was 'panic at the Treasury as Gladstone goes MISSING prompting frantic search' after an email was sent to civil servants asking if they had seen him. He was, thankfully, quickly found and an update was later posted on Instagram: 'Lots of speculation about my whereabouts this weekend. Obviously I couldn't possibly comment… #catsontour.'

Gladstone fans could even follow his travels around the corridors of power: on one occasion a small camera was attached to his collar, allowing viewers to enjoy a cat's-eye view of the Treasury.

In terms of his main role, Gladstone was quickly dubbed 'a cold blooded killer' by one Downing Street insider, who observed that 'the bodies are piling up'. He caught his first unfortunate victim within forty-eight hours of moving into his new home, with a further six casualties over the next three months.

In September 2017, civil servants created a chart outlining Gladstone's kills, which revealed he had dispatched twenty-two mice and two flies.

Gladstone continued to 'post' on Instagram, including some maths problems for children on National Numeracy Day. His updates continued until February 2020, when his followers were told to head to the main Treasury Instagram account for more Gladstone pictures.

While on social media, he congratulated Team GB in the 2016 Olympics and celebrated International Cat Day, St George's Day, Christmas and various fiscal events such as the Budget. On International Women's Day 2018, Gladstone was pictured sat on a green, white and purple flag with a caption reading, 'I don't see gender. I just see treats.'

In January 2020, just before the coronavirus pandemic fully hit, Gladstone announced online that, like much of the population, his working life was also undergoing a major change. 'I've had such a restful holiday with one of my #HMTreasury humans that I'm going to be working from my new home for a while,' the post read. 'It seems I've made such good progress as chief mouser that I can relax a bit for a while and try out this remote working thing.'

'We know that Gladstone wasn't a posh boy,' says cat behaviourist Celia Haddon.

> Gladstone's life before Battersea was on the streets living rough as a stray. Black cats are sometimes less popular than other cats, so I feel the Treasury did the right thing in giving an all-black cat a chance.

By all accounts, Gladstone was a good mouser, but living in an office might not suit all cats – lots of humans coming and going might be stressful for cats that have not had the right upbringing. Cats that are going to live surrounded by lots of humans need a kittenhood where they can get used to frequent human interactions and movements.

Battersea wouldn't have known how Gladstone's kittenhood had gone, but perhaps they chose slightly the wrong cat for the civil service environment. Not all cats are cuddle bunnies. And not all cats welcome human strangers frequently in their territory. Maybe Gladstone didn't have enough privacy in his office life.

Sonia Khan worked as a civil servant in the Treasury press office and then as a special adviser, on the political side, to two Chancellors, Philip Hammond and Sajid Javid.

'Gladstone had a home on the second floor in the Treasury building,' remembers Khan.

A few young members of the staff looked after him and he had a bed and a mini home there with his snacks and toys. There used to be a sign asking people not to disturb him if he was there, but he didn't often go roaming or exploring in the same way as some of the other cats. So I think there was quite an early sense that, actually, maybe the life of Whitehall wasn't quite right for him.

When I worked for Philip [Hammond] we thought about getting the cat in the Christmas photo, but he wasn't very cooperative with those kinds of things. So we ended up using

Philip's dogs. There is always a battle for the best Christmas photo, and the animals are always a winner because, regardless of what people think about politicians, you can't say a bad word about the animals. It was more difficult with Sajid [Javid] when he moved into the Treasury, as he had an allergy to cats, so he actually couldn't get very close.

I don't think Gladstone went outside very often, even though the Treasury has a great courtyard. And I think he just found it quite stressful, the constant hustle and the busyness, also that the lights are very bright and white, and often give the humans headaches. So I wouldn't be surprised if it didn't work for him.

Another senior Treasury insider, who had a large degree of experience with Gladstone, was less charitable. She told me simply, 'He was a jerk!'

When it became clear Gladstone was not adjusting to his new life particularly well, his Treasury keepers decided a change of scenery might help him, as Khan explains:

> I remember he went on a mini holiday or a break at one stage, just to see if he would be better in a different environment. A member of staff took him to the countryside for a bit, somewhere with lots of green space and grass and a bit more room to roam. He thrived there. He came back and we realised that it wasn't working with him, so it was agreed that he would step away from his desk duties and be looked after by a member of staff permanently.
>
> He was definitely a night owl and probably an introvert,

I think, who liked to wander with few people around. So it was quite nice to see him when I was working late and putting together something that wasn't very fun or dealing with a negative issue. But it was very much Gladstone saying: 'On my terms, I come to see you. You don't come to see me, Sonia.'

Both Khan and I very much enjoyed working alongside Gladstone, but it's clear his destiny lay outside the Treasury.

One Downing Street insider from the time puts it more bluntly to *Political Animals*: 'Gladstone got depression and was parcelled out of Whitehall under the civil service PR spin of "working from home" (that old chestnut).'

Whatever the case, Whitehall life really wasn't for Gladstone, so it's only right and proper that he now enjoys a more traditional cat lifestyle, happily in the care of one of the civil servants who worked alongside him.

PART IV

THE POLITICAL ANIMALS OF DOWNING STREET

CHAPTER NINE

POLITICAL ANIMALS AT NO. 11

After the demise of Humphrey, there wasn't another cat in Downing Street under the Blairs, despite the promises of Alastair Campbell's press office. It wasn't until Gordon Brown's administration, in the late 2000s, that another feline prowled the building. This time, it belonged to the Chancellor, Alistair Darling, and his wife, Maggie.

The Darlings brought their cat Sybil south from Edinburgh to London not long after they moved into the flat above No. 10 that has been the home of recent Chancellors and their families. Though traditionally Prime Ministers lived 'above the shop' at No. 10, with the Chancellor installed above No. 11, premiers since Sir Tony Blair have usually preferred to live in the larger No. 11 flat, with the exception of Rishi Sunak, who was allocated the smaller No. 10 flat as Chancellor and opted to return there as Prime Minister. Shortly after she arrived, a No. 10 spokesman confirmed that Sybil, the Darlings' cat, would be allowed to roam all of Downing Street: 'It's in the nature of things that cats are difficult to confine.' Named after the *Fawlty Towers* character, Sybil was a family cat rather than the nation's chief mouser; nonetheless, she was renowned for her rodent-catching skills. A Treasury spokesman lauded Sybil as 'a confirmed mouser'.

Rumours that Gordon Brown and his wife did not like Sybil

were denied by his spokesman at the time, who said: 'The Prime Minister and Sarah do not have a problem with it.'

The public certainly liked Sybil. She received so much fan mail – from humans and cats alike – that the Darlings paid for printed cards with Sybil's paw print and a photograph to be sent to the cat's well-wishers.

Behind closed doors, however, Sybil wasn't always well-behaved, as a Downing Street insider from the time reveals to *Political Animals*: 'At one Cabinet meeting Alistair Darling was somewhat bemused to see Jacqui Smith, the then Home Secretary, making faces at him. He wasn't at all pleased when he followed her gaze and saw Sybil leaving an unwelcome deposit under the Cabinet table.'

Overall, life in Downing Street did not suit Sybil. When the Darlings made their frequent trips to Edinburgh for Alistair's constituency work, Sybil stayed at the home of a senior civil servant who worked closely with the Chancellor, the late Chris Martin, and his wife, Christina Scott. This was, of course, better than Sybil staying in Downing Street without proper company – the buildings have staff 24/7 but are usually very empty at weekends – as there was a worry Sybil would be lonely in the flat. A friend of the Chancellor told the *Daily Telegraph*, 'Sybil didn't like being confined, so it was thought best that she went to stay with friends. The Darlings had hoped at some point to have her back in Edinburgh.' Eventually, Martin and Scott adopted Sybil from the Darlings. The cat lived happily in her new home until she died peacefully, after a short illness, in July 2009.

Though Larry arrived at 10 Downing Street in 2011, it wasn't until 2012 that a Chancellor's cat returned to No. 11. Freya lived there for four years as the Osborne family's pet. The handsome tabby, who had very large whiskers, had been with the family at their home in Notting Hill in north-west London. Her arrival at Downing Street was unexpected, not least by George Osborne, who thought she was lost.

Freya had gone missing in 2009 but was found alive and well in 2012, having lived as a stray in a garden not far from her original home. She had been looked after and fed by a neighbour of the Osbornes who had not seen the posters the family had put up to try to find Freya when she first went missing. Freya was microchipped, so, when scanned by a vet, the mystery of her provenance was solved. She was returned to her family and joined them in her new Downing Street home.

Larry is and always has been a notoriously bad mouser (see Chapter Eleven). Once, entering his office in No. 10, David Cameron found Larry asleep in his chair as a mouse nonchalantly ran across the room. When the Prime Minister awakened Larry to try to cajole him into catching the mouse, the cat opened one eye and did not move another muscle. Freya and Larry therefore had a 'job share' as chief mouser; however, an adviser who worked in Downing Street at the time tells me the two cats did not get on, with Freya often 'knocking seven bells out of Larry' (see photo section). Another Downing Street insider remembers 'Freya being a real presence strutting around No. 10. Larry, on the other hand, was a committed napper.'

Freya was not the only Osborne pet who made bids for freedom: the family hamster also escaped on one occasion. According to Osborne, 'My family were terrified this hamster was going to start appearing in press conferences with the Prime Minister, or that maybe when Barack Obama visits, suddenly the hamster would run across the room. So we spent about two weeks searching for this hamster, and then finally Freya found it.'

In December 2013, the Osbornes brought Lola the bichon frisé into their home. Osborne tweeted of Lola: 'Some early issues with toilet training… but we don't care. We love her.' Lola later 'married' Osborne's fellow Cabinet minister Michael Gove's male bichon frisé, Snowy, in a 'ceremony' strewn with flowers.

Freya was nothing if not intrepid. Oliver Wright, a journalist who worked for *The Independent*, told his paper that Freya was known to wander:

> She has been found in the most secure area of the Foreign Office, inside the room in No. 10 where the Cabinet meets and trying to seek entry into the Treasury. She was even caught by Mr Osborne inside his red box.
>
> On many an evening she can be found in Westminster's favoured political watering hole, the Red Lion – despite having to cross four lanes of traffic to get there. Apparently, at the end of the evening, the barmaids regularly have to carry her back home.

Claims Freya and Lola did not get on were denied. But Freya's wide wanderings proved problematic, with her frequently roaming around the busy central London environs of Downing Street. Kate Jones, who worked with homeless people, once came across Freya wandering about a mile and a half from home and rang the number on her collar, only to be told that Freya's home was Downing Street. Before the cat was brought home by a driver,

Jones took a photograph with Freya and posted it online with the caption: 'Found – on the streets of Vauxhall. Not everyone is as lucky as Freya. George [Osborne] please stop cutting homeless services.'

She later told the *Daily Telegraph*, 'I did find it slightly ironic that I had been up at 5 a.m. trying to help twenty-four people who had been sleeping rough in Newham and we couldn't find anywhere to send them, then this cat gets chauffeur-driven home.'

In August 2014, Freya had an accident near Downing Street in which she was clipped by a car. Thankfully, her injuries were not fatal, but the decision was made to rehome her somewhere less hazardous for the curious moggy and with more space to explore. She initially lived with a member of the household staff and then one of the Downing Street butlers. She was much loved by her new owners and eventually she died peacefully.

Lola remained at Downing Street with the Osbornes, having seen off Freya. She had her fans too. On her arrival at Downing Street, a pet owners' lifestyle website, PetsPyjamas, sent Lola a congratulatory gift basket. Osborne sent back a note 'written' by Lola:

Dear PetsPyjamas,

Thank you so much for the wonderful hamper of my dreams. It was filled with everything a Lola could want! The cracker is wonderful, and no matter how often I chew and pull it, I always get a surprise when I find the treat! The bandana is super stylish and all the other pups are jealous of me! I heard the word 'edible card', and though I haven't found what it is yet, I think it'll be lovely. The box is great too, and I can't stop staring at myself. Thank you, and thank you again,

Woof! Lola Osborne

In 2019, when Boris Johnson became Prime Minister, he brought his dog Dilyn with him to No. 10. At the time, Osborne reflected in *The Spectator*:

> Dilyn the Jack Russell has moved into Downing Street. Lola, our bichon frisé, got there first. Her excitement when I got home at the end of a long day was a treat. The start of the days, however, weren't so rewarding. The flats are at the top of the buildings. The garden is at the bottom. At 6 a.m. you could find me walking around it with Lola, waiting for her to do her business. Sometimes David [Cameron, then Prime Minister] would be watching amused from his kitchen window, no doubt making sure I picked up after her. I wonder who takes Dilyn down to the garden in the morning? Boris is good at creating a mess but perhaps not so good at cleaning it up.

Osborne's successor Philip Hammond (now Lord Hammond), who served under Theresa May, had two dogs, Rex, a Welsh terrier, and Oscar, a wire-haired dachshund. Susan Williams-Walker, Hammond's wife, ran an Instagram account for Rex, featuring photos of him walking and relaxing in the family's home in the Surrey constituency of Runnymede and Weybridge, which was Hammond's constituency between 1997 and 2019. The account bio read, 'I'm a Welsh Terrier called Rex with a newly acquired canine brother but I'm still the King of my household! I love walking, shopping and eating out!' In 2015, when Hammond was Foreign Secretary, a post from 'Rex' saw the dog alongside a poster supporting the #StopYulin campaign, in opposition to the annual dog meat and lychee festival in Yulin, China.

In May 2017, Williams-Walker was asked by the *Evening Standard* whether Rex and Oscar were getting on with Larry. 'No, not really,' she said. 'There was a story about how the dogs are scared of the cats. But Rex is a terrier, I'm not sure he's scared of anything. He goes after the cats … All of them. It's mostly Larry. He usually stands his ground.'

For a number of years, the Hammond and Williams-Walker family Christmas cards featured Rex and Oscar in playful poses. In December 2016, shortly after the two dogs moved into Downing Street, they posed outside the door of No. 11, but this was a rare outing for the pooches, as they had been kept in the flat to avoid Larry.

Much more prominent, at least on social media, was Bailey the cavapoo, who lived in No. 11 with Sajid Javid when he was Chancellor. Javid had run for leader of the Conservatives against Boris Johnson in 2019, and Bailey was a big part of his campaign videos. Javid and Bailey were filmed together as Javid made tea and Marmite on toast and his wife Laura and their children waved them both off for a day's campaigning.

Gareth Milner, who ran the digital side of Sajid Javid's leadership campaign, tells *Political Animals* that Bailey was an invaluable part of the team.

Bailey's star turn was part of a campaign video said by the *Daily Mail* to be 'the best of the leadership battle so far'. She was a natural and much-loved part of Sajid's family, but what we didn't expect was the extent that a few brief shots of Bailey barking and playing with a ball would take off in the national press. What the cutting room floor robbed the world of in the edit was a number of shots of Bailey looking longingly, lovingly and adoringly at her family, and perhaps at some food on the table as well.

I can vouch that during my time working on the 2019 leadership campaign Bailey was a very friendly and personable dog, one I was glad to know before she became famous and moved into Downing Street when Sajid was appointed as Boris Johnson's Chancellor.

Bailey was soon joined by the Johnsons' dog Dilyn. Alas, Dilyn displayed amorous intentions towards his new neighbour. Various newspapers reported how Dilyn could not be trusted on his own around Bailey and had to be pulled off her several times in the Downing Street garden.

Bailey clashed with Larry in August 2019, resulting in a serious fight. A source told the *Daily Mail* at the time, 'Bailey started it but Larry definitely finished it.' In an interview with LBC radio in September 2019, Javid said, 'Larry is a bit territorial, I've got to say. He's a good cat, but he does like to pick on the dogs.'

Amid the chaotic politics of 2022, Larry must have been wondering whether both his human and his animal companions were coming or going, with four Chancellors in four months. Neither Nadhim Zahawi – who was very fond of Evie and Ossie when he was at the Cabinet Office – nor his successor Kwasi Kwarteng had animals during their short tenures in Downing

Street, although the Sunaks did have Nova the dog when Rishi Sunak was Chancellor. However, Poppy the Labrador lived at 11 Downing Street between October 2022 and July 2024, when Sir Jeremy Hunt was in post. Under Liz Truss, Poppy was the only dog in Downing Street, but when Truss resigned and was succeeded as Prime Minister by Rishi Sunak, Nova returned with her family (see Chapter Ten).

Although Nova and Poppy shared the interlinked space of the Downing Street buildings, it appears Poppy was top dog. 'Poppy was rather overwhelming for Nova, who was quite a nervous dog,' Hunt tells *Political Animals*. 'But they got along well and were happy to have playdates in the Downing Street garden. Larry, however, was a different kettle of fish: fiercely territorial, he would scowl and hiss at any other animals who came near his space around the No. 10 front door.'

A Downing Street insider who works there to this day agrees with this assessment, remembering the Hunt and Sunak dogs getting on, being well behaved and keeping a relatively low profile, with all acknowledging that Larry was really in charge.

> I remember Jeremy Hunt's and Rishi's dogs; they were lovely. They spent most of their time in the residences and when they came out into the main building it was usually because they were heading for a walk in the park and absolutely not to roam the house, because of Larry! Both the Hunts and the Sunaks were very respectful of his territory, which was very kind of them both. Their families are lovely people. The dogs were very well behaved too – friendly dogs who were always keen to offer you a lick!

There are many receptions hosted at Downing Street in the state rooms or the garden as part of the work of government. I have attended quite a few of these as a special adviser and now as a journalist. Poppy proved very popular with guests at these events, despite Hunt's initial reservations: 'We were always nervous about letting Poppy join our receptions in case there were people with allergies to dog hair, but in the end we just risked it because it was such a hit for guests to see her in the No. 11 state room.'

Lots of people think politicians are lazy – and some are – but it's virtually impossible not to work very hard indeed if you are in any job in Downing Street. Sir Jeremy, a keen runner who has completed many marathons for charity, used exercise to escape from the pressure of high office. 'The best part of my day was taking Poppy for a run first thing around St James's Park and Hyde Park. That was when I came up with the best lines for my Budget speeches. So she was definitely a Chancellor's best friend.'

Hunt also entered Poppy in the Westminster Dog of the Year competition a number of times, coming third in 2021. In 2023, he told his local newspaper, the *Farnham Herald*:

> Poppy has changed our family dynamic in a fantastic way, not least for our children, who adore her. She's brought so much joy to our lives, especially since moving into No. 11, even if she is a bit of competition for Larry the Cat!
>
> She has taken to the political lifestyle perfectly thanks to her inquisitive, friendly and lively nature, and always wanting to be in the thick of it. She is a worthy contender for the Westminster Dog of the Year title because she is a huge character as well as the most important member of our family!

As an MP in the marginal seat of Godalming and Ash (formerly South West Surrey) since 2005, Sir Jeremy knows that every part of a parliamentarian's image and pursuits can make a difference. In the 2024 election, his majority was a slim 891:

> I guess I figured that there may be lots of dog lovers in a marginal seat, but I doubt it helped much. That said, when I walked out of Downing Street with Poppy on the morning after the election, someone tweeted: 'He's got a Labrador. Can I change the way I voted?'

That walk from Downing Street with his wife Lucia, their three children and Poppy was captured by cameras. One of these was my Westminster lobby colleague Chris Hope, political editor of GB News. As Hunt passed, he said to his family – garnering a laugh from Hope – 'That is Mr Hope – a nice guy. Don't believe what they say about him. He's actually all right!'

Given the close scrutiny politicians are under these days, they are usually keen to keep their children out of the limelight. For instance, Sir Keir Starmer has a teenage son and daughter but has never confirmed their names or been publicly photographed with them for political purposes. As I know from working very closely with four Cabinet ministers during my three and a half years as a special adviser, politicians have all the same dilemmas with naughty children, rows with their spouses, financial concerns and everything else that adults deal with as part of life. Having been on the inside of politics, I am delighted when I see politicians with animals, given that it is another 'normal' aspect of family life politicians can enjoy and embrace. It's also an aspect of their private life that can easily be public, with little risk and often some reward. Hunt agrees: 'It does humanise us if it is done authentically. But the most important way to be human is for us as a class to talk more naturally and not be perceived as constantly spouting the party line or attacking our opponents.'

Rachel Reeves, who became Chancellor in July 2024, is a cat person like her boss, Sir Keir Starmer, but perhaps for more practical purposes than simply loving the felines. 'There is a reason why everyone in this building has cats,' she told Sky News in March 2025. 'There's definitely a mouse problem in Downing Street, so yeah, I prefer cats to mice.'

The acquisition of Pumpkin the rescue kitten came after lobbying from Reeves's children. Pumpkin moved into Downing Street with Reeves, her husband Nicholas Joicey, a senior civil servant, and their two children. 'I held out for eleven and a bit years of being a mum to get a pet. We had a couple of fish before, but they didn't survive,' she said.

Reeves mentioned Pumpkin on BBC 5 Live in October 2024 and was asked by presenter Matt Chorley, 'Quite a seasonal name, will it still work in the spring?' She quipped, 'Pumpkin is for life, not just for Halloween.'

'It's a little rescue kitten,' she told Sky News.

I've actually really taken to it. During the Budget, it was obviously a massive week for me, because I was left alone with the cat while my husband took the kids away for half-term. So I know everyone thinks the Budget was a big moment, but it's actually keeping a kitten alive for a week as someone who has never had any responsibility for pets before really. It was quite a busy week, but I managed to pop up and make sure that the cat was fed.

Speaking of the mice problem in her family's flat, Reeves said: 'I mean they were just everywhere. But not any more. The cat has done a good job.'

Both Pumpkin and the Starmers' two cats, Jojo and Prince, are now kept away from Larry entirely, due to Larry's elder statesman status, territorial ways and history of frequent clashes with other cats. Downing Street insiders have revealed to me that a little ladder has been constructed from the flats to the garden so the cats can get out to exercise, laze and do their business. Given their earlier clashes with Larry – and Larry's advancing years – it's thought that allowing him his own territory and keeping the other cats in their respective flats makes more sense.

And perhaps it also represents Larry's ultimate victory as Downing Street's top cat.

CHAPTER TEN

ONE PRIME MINISTER (AND CHANCELLOR) ON HIS DOG: RISHI SUNAK ON NOVA

With the politically choppy waters of recent years, Nova, the Sunaks' fox red Labrador retriever, is one of the few family animals to have spent any length of time in Downing Street. She arrived in June 2021.

By a quirk of the building's layout, the two flats that the Prime Minister and Chancellor live in with their families have often been swapped since the time of Sir Tony Blair's administration, as we saw in Chapter Nine. The No. 11 flat is larger, so the Blair family lived there, with Gordon Brown in the smaller No. 10 residence. Downing Street is all interlinked anyway, so it's perfectly natural to walk 'through' the houses; the press office is in No. 12, for instance, down the corridor from the Prime Minister's office in No. 10. With his family having happy memories of their time in the smaller No. 10 flat when he served as Chancellor, Sunak opted to return there as Prime Minister, rather than moving into the larger residence above No. 11 that had been used by recent premiers.

But, as Sunak tells *Political Animals*, it was a little bit of a battle to get the dog in the first place. 'I was the last person, the last domino to fall in the family,' he recalls. Perhaps unsurprisingly, Sunak's two daughters, Anoushka and Krishna, were the most enthusiastic.

The girls went there first in wanting a dog, obviously. And then what happened is my wife switched sides, and then it was three against one. Essentially they all said to me, 'Well, you're never around anyway.' So as an absentee dad and an absentee husband, I basically had no moral authority on these types of things.

In the American TV drama about life in the White House, *The West Wing*, President Jed Bartlet is a Nobel Prize-winning economist. When staff urge him to act, his catchphrase is: 'Show me numbers.' Having worked with Rishi Sunak way back when he was a junior minister in the Ministry of Housing, Communities and Local Government in 2018 and 2019, when I was advising his boss, the Secretary of State, James Brokenshire, I know Sunak can be persuaded by facts and figures. Anoushka Sunak knew this too.

My eldest daughter made a PowerPoint presentation about why we should get a dog. It was a lot about why it would be good for teaching them [the children] responsibility. She found something saying it's good for family too.

We are not small-dog people. We all love Labradors – they're kind of idiot-proof, family friendly. But given we are informed by our Yorkshire life and our Yorkshire home, we have a fox red Lab, [a breed] which is very rare in London but in the country is very common because they're working dogs.

Despite his many political priorities, Sunak was determined Nova's arrival would be managed by him in the right way. 'I read all the books. I have a whole library. The first few nights Nova was with us, I slept on the couch in the kitchen in the No. 10 flat. She had to be crate-trained.' This is a form of positive training in which the dog is given a crate or cage to feel comfortable in, to sleep in and to make sure they are relaxed in a new environment. Despite being one of the busiest and most powerful politicians in the country, Sunak was determined to make sure Nova settled in.

> Crate training is good for her independence, but it can be tough. You've just taken this little puppy away from its mum. My team in the office knew in these few first days I needed to be able to run up and down from the flat. So I slept on the sofa. And I think on the third night, actually, my wife came in and was like: 'You literally did not even do this for our own children. You put them in the room and did the hardcore thing and told them to get on with it. You were not sleeping on the couch outside their room! Come back to bed and stop this nonsense!'

Nova proved a hit in Downing Street and was fussed over by civil servants, advisers, other politicians and visiting dignitaries, including Vice-President Kamala Harris, who had dinner with the Sunaks in the No. 10 flat.

'Nova kind of grew up in Downing Street, so she got massively spoiled by everyone,' says Sunak.

> She used to bark at Paul the gardener's rake, which she found very weird and stressful. She'd get very perturbed by it. And then ultimately she loved him and loved the garden. Obviously

it's a very lovely place for her and that's where she got trained to do everything, in that garden.

Unlike most homes, Downing Street has a lift, which Sunak would use each morning to take Nova outside for her walk. She was particularly cautious coming out of the lift, looking from side to side each time, double checking that a certain resident of Downing Street was not around.

> She's petrified of Larry. He's not the friendliest of cats. He would hiss at her when she was a little puppy. She was terrified of him then. But what is funny is she maintained that fear of him even though she became three times his size.
> If the elevator ever opened on the ground floor, which is kind of where Larry is, behind the black door, she wouldn't get out straight away, because she knew that's his domain. So she would never just scamper out. Whereas, if she was going to the basement, where the garden and the cars are, she would just run out. But on the ground floor, even as a fully grown Labrador, it's like she was saying, 'Where's that cat?'

Unlike the more boisterous Dilyn, so beloved of Boris Johnson, Nova was a more low-key animal, although she had her moments. One in particular caused international press attention.

In March 2023, Sunak and his wife Akshata Murty were walking Nova, then two years old, around the edge of the Serpentine lake in Hyde Park. She was off the lead in an area where there were signs stating she should have been on it. A police officer spoke to Murty about this and reminded her of the rules, but the whole incident was captured by an onlooker and posted on TikTok. Sunak recalls, 'Someone had left a bunch of sandwiches on the ground and Nova ran for them. And then there was literally a national incident because it was on TikTok. You let your dog misbehave for five seconds!'

More positively, Nova was a frequent attender at Lessons at 10, an initiative set up by Murty in which pupils came to Downing Street to learn in the historic surroundings of the building. The scheme aimed to bring education to life, encourage a love of learning and inspire children from across the UK. Sunak popped in when he could, but Nova was the star attraction, delighting children and adding a fun element to their unforgettable day in Downing Street.

Nova was also very well behaved on an important occasion early in Sunak's administration. 'The week after I became Prime Minister, we launched the poppy appeal on Downing Street and she came out with us. She was quite young, wearing a little poppy. I remember she just sat there very nicely, did what she was meant to do, then went back inside. Brilliant.'

Nova was also a hit with US First Lady Dr Jill Biden and other attendees of the coronation tea party held in honour of King Charles III in May 2023: 'We had bunting up everywhere. It's literally one of our favourite days when we were in Downing Street ... it was really fun. Nova was just kind of running around outside, everyone giving her too many sandwiches!'

Nova also frequently attended Downing Street receptions, the near-daily events in which the Prime Minister entertains charities, organisations and other politicians.

Amid the frantic pace of life as Chancellor and then Prime Minister, the famously workaholic Sunak says Nova helped him relax, get some exercise and take a bit of time away from the coalface.

> I love going for walks. I find they help you clear your head. And Nova meant that I could just go for a walk on my own and no one would think 'that's a bit strange', because I had a dog to walk. I do a lot of that in Yorkshire; she's a proper North Yorkshire dog.

Nova's very different upbringing in Downing Street meant she took a little time to adjust when the Sunaks moved out in 2024. A valued and much-loved member of the Sunak family, she still accompanies them when they go to Rishi Sunak's Yorkshire constituency of Richmond. 'Nova does a commute every week to Yorkshire, so everyone on the LNER train knows her. The team there are very good with her. She gets a lot of attention.'

Nova's love of the countryside and having space to roam was cemented in Chequers, the Prime Minister's country residence in Buckinghamshire.

> She would find her own way to the Chequers kitchen whenever we were there. We would wonder, 'Where's the dog gone?' and she would have slinked off down to the kitchen, where they would be giving her vegetables and things that they were cooking. And she'd be extremely jolly.
>
> The team at Chequers really loved her because she's a well-behaved dog that didn't damage anything. She was very appreciated.

Sunak says that last part diplomatically, pointedly not making any reference to the Johnsons' often badly behaved dog Dilyn (see Chapter Twelve).

'Whenever we had our Sunday roast at Chequers, it was a treat for her too. We would do a little mini Sunday roast that they would put down beside the table, just for her.'

Back in London, notwithstanding her fear of Larry, Nova got on well with the other dogs of Downing Street, including Dilyn and latterly Sir Jeremy Hunt's dog, Poppy. 'They did run around together quite a bit. She's quite a docile thing, Nova. She's not very aggressive. She's kind of meek.

'It is nice, you know,' says Sunak. 'Who doesn't love dogs?'

CHAPTER ELEVEN

LARRY, KING OF DOWNING STREET

On a cold, dark, wet Sunday in January 2011, the BBC's political correspondent Gary O'Donoghue was broadcasting live from Downing Street. But on that particular night, the eyes of the nation were not on him. O'Donoghue's words about a speech by Prime Minister David Cameron are long forgotten, as would be the broadcast if it were not for one uninvited guest in the background. Over the veteran journalist's right shoulder, scurrying past the famous black door of No. 10, was the unmistakable silhouette of a rat.

'The cameraman, the producer and I were the only people in Downing Street that night,' says O'Donoghue.

> It was deserted. It was pitch black. I was completely oblivious to it. And then the cameraman said afterwards he thought there was a pretty big rat in the shot. We looked back at the recording and it actually was there live on the *News at Ten* on a Sunday night. The footage kind of went all over the place. It was on YouTube straight away. Someone said to me they saw it on Russian TV! Most bizarre.

Little did O'Donoghue know, his broadcast was to be a notable one not only in terms of its worldwide reach and notoriety to this day but also in regard to the chain of events it triggered just yards away, behind 10 Downing Street's black door.

As seasoned operatives such as Liz Sugg, David Cameron's senior special adviser and head of operations and visits, know well, getting things done in the political world is all about timing. For some time, Sugg and a small band of true believers inside 10 Downing Street had been pushing to adopt a new cat. Sybil, Alistair and Maggie Darling's cat, had left a couple of years previously and the vermin problem still loomed large. Eight months into the Cameron administration, helped by the rat-related media furore, Sugg knew it was her time to strike. In her first extensive interview about Larry, she tells *Political Animals*:

> The very next morning, we thought, right, this is our moment. We rang up Battersea Dogs & Cats home and said, 'We're calling from Downing Street. We'd like to get a cat. Would you be interested in helping us?' And, funnily enough, they said, 'Yes, absolutely.' So I got a little group together, making sure it was across the civil service as well as on the political side of things.
>
> We'd tested the water a few times to see whether or not the house would accept a cat. And I think it's fair to say there was a kind of pro-cat faction and an anti-cat faction. But it was never top of the priority list, obviously, and it fell by the wayside. There were mice running around all the time.
>
> There were always people who had a problem with the idea of a Downing Street cat, asking, 'Who's going to look after it, where will it go to the loo? Who's going to let it in and out? What if the cat gets trapped?' They said, 'It's not appropriate, because it's such a busy house, with so many people working there. Inside,

it's not really set up like a modern office. Who's going to pay for it? It can't be on the taxpayer.' That rumbled on for a while.

Then came O'Donoghue's broadcast.

'We slightly bounced the anti-cat faction into it,' reflects Sugg. 'I'd spoken to the Prime Minister about it and he gave his blessing. So we went off to Battersea and I was hoping that we'd get a cute little kitten.'

But Battersea staff explained to Sugg and her group that the kitten they had in mind might not fit in with the workings of Downing Street. The cat's welfare was, obviously, Battersea's priority. Sugg explained the set-up of Downing Street, how

> the door opens and closes, the number of people who come through it, the number of events and state visits and dinners and the working environment.
>
> So they said, 'Our recommendation is that you get a cat who knows his stuff and is a bit streetwise and isn't going to be scared, because the last thing we want is for the cat to be unhappy there.'
>
> And then Larry walked up to us. He came up and pushed his nose against my leg, so I gave him a little stroke. And all of us who were there fell in love with him.

Larry had been found on the streets of Wandsworth in south London. He was a young cat, somewhere between three and five years old. But his stay in Battersea was to be a brief one, having been rescued just a few weeks before Sugg and her group made Larry their instant choice. 'We were keen to get a rescue cat – not only is it a good thing to do, it would also be a high-profile way to promote that there are always plenty of rescue cats in need of a home,' says Sugg.

Soon after the Battersea visit, staff from the rescue centre travelled the two and a half miles to Downing Street. They inspected where Larry would sleep and made sure plans were in place for him to be looked after properly.

Everyone who needed to be was happy – including Cameron. 'We came back and told the Prime Minister and showed him a photo and said, "This is Larry. He's going to come and live with us, if that's all right with you?" He agreed,' says Sugg.

Larry arrived on 15 January 2011, a month after O'Donoghue's broadcast. The headlines on the Downing Street website that day read, 'Prime Minister's meeting with Russian foreign secretary Lavrov, Alternative Vote Bill, Ministry of Defence email sackings, inflation and Larry the cat'. In a statement, Cameron said, 'I'm delighted to welcome Larry to his new home. He came highly recommended to me by Battersea Dogs & Cats Home, who did a fantastic job looking after him. I'm sure he will be a great addition to Downing Street and will charm our many visitors.'

Sugg was delighted she finally had the cat at Downing Street that she had been campaigning for. Understandably, Battersea were keen to have their moment in the sun too.

> I think Battersea might have tipped the media off. We thought, 'Let's just get him in and make it as non-traumatic for the cat as possible, poor thing.' But they arrived, opened the van door and took him out on the side of the photographers on

the street. And obviously they [the press] were very excited about it.

In a press release at that time, Battersea called Larry 'a great match [for Downing Street], because he is a very sociable cat who enjoys attention and loves human contact'. He was also, they said, 'a bit of a bruiser'.

'He just moved in and made himself at home,' says Sugg. 'He found his favourite little seat inside on the windowsill by the front door, because it's directly above a radiator.'

From day one, the media had huge interest in Larry, and he took all the attention largely in his stride, with the exception of scratching a female reporter, who had attempted to pick him up, while he struggled to break free of her arms. Within hours, Larry was a global celebrity, photos and videos of him flying around the world. Twitter accounts were set up, too, all claiming to be the cat's official account.

'The public loved Larry,' Sugg recalls.

> We got all sorts of presents sent in. I remember a blanket with Larry's name on it. We put that on the windowsill and it became his favourite blanket.
>
> When the PM's daughter Florence was born, very early on into his premiership, there was a lovely reaction. Lots of people sent in crochet blankets and little presents for her, but I think we had more gifts for Larry than for the Prime Minister's daughter!
>
> Obviously everyone wanted to get a cat after we got Larry. Palmerston, Gladstone, they were copycats. It's not every

workplace that can really have a cat, but given that there are people at Downing Street 24/7, the brilliant doorkeepers and the security guys, then it's possible. They all fell in love with him as well – well, most of them! Larry learned that someone's going to open the door for him if he waits there long enough. It worked out pretty well for Larry, I think.

He is a good cat. He never went to the loo in an inappropriate place, which was quite lucky. That's what I was a bit worried about. Those who didn't like him avoided him.

And Larry was definitely a Larry. 'There was a conversation at the start about whether he should be renamed. Some people said, "Let's call him Winston or Churchill" or something like that. But I said his name's Larry, it suits him. We can't change his name. So he stayed as Larry,' says Sugg.

Larry is of course a shorter version of the name Lawrence, which means 'laurel-crowned'. And given the cat's high status as the nation's best-known pest controller, it's a fitting name for the chief mouser, I think we can all agree.

There were concerns, though, about a rescue cat coming to Downing Street, being so high-profile so quickly and whether someone would try to claim the stray, says Sugg. 'I was worried that someone would say that he was theirs. For the first month or so I thought we shouldn't get too attached, in case suddenly someone said, "That's my long-lost cat. You've stolen him." But it never happened.'

Loved as Larry was by his new friends at Downing Street, looming large was the slight problem of him failing to execute the practicalities of his new job: chief mouser to the Cabinet Office at 10 Downing Street.

To make matters worse, the spin operation at Downing Street had declared that Larry was 'a good ratter' with 'a high chase-drive and hunting instinct' developed during his time wandering the streets. A spokesman said that Larry showed 'a very strong predatory drive' and was already playing with toy mice hours into his time in Downing Street. As a former special adviser myself, this is very much the sort of partially true angle I would have slipped into the public domain to try to big up Larry. Well-intentioned though it may have been, it wasn't entirely followed through by its subject. Not for the first time in politics, a promise was made that wasn't quite kept.

In fairness to Downing Street, they weren't the only ones hyping up Larry's talents. Battersea also told the media, 'There are usually tell-tale signs of the hunter instinct from a previous life in some cats and even in the cattery, Larry showed those signs.'

Perhaps learning the lessons of their early enthusiasm for Larry's mousing skills, the Downing Street website now tacitly acknowledges that he is perhaps not the best at this activity, despite being the first cat to officially have the title.

> Larry has been in residence since 15 February 2011. He is the first cat at No. 10 to be bestowed with the official title Chief Mouser ... Larry spends his days greeting guests to the house, inspecting security defences and testing antique furniture for napping quality. His day-to-day responsibilities also include

contemplating a solution to the mouse occupancy of the house. Larry says this is still 'in the tactical planning stage'.

But Larry has, in fact, caught mice. In late April 2011, Larry climbed through the window of Downing Street with a rodent in his jaws and proudly dropped it at the feet of some of the secretaries working for the Prime Minister. After their initial shock passed, everyone cheered, as he had finally done the job he'd been brought in to do. Two months later, in June, Cameron reported Larry had caught two more mice.

'Larry has never been the best mouser,' admits Sugg. 'I think there's a few photos of him playing around with a mouse, but his very presence meant there were fewer mice running around the building – so mission accomplished. I think the smell of him put them off, even if he didn't actually catch many!'

As cat expert Celia Haddon explains:

> Not all cats are interested in hunting, either because they just haven't needed to or because they have not had the chance to do it. Cameron should have thought himself lucky that Larry didn't spend his time bringing in half-dead rats that would then be hunted around the Cabinet Office floor. People who get a cat often find they have more, rather than fewer, mice in their house.

'I mean, he does catch mice, I've seen him' says one of Larry's greatest friends and defenders Justin Ng, who has taken probably thousands of photos of the tabby while working on Downing Street as a photojournalist.

People say he's not a good mouser, but there have been a few occasions where he has. But because he's a bit fat, he's a bit slow, he just doesn't have quite the quickness. One Christmas Eve he pounced on a pigeon, but he didn't kill it. Just trying to show you, you know: "I'm the boss. I'm playing with you here." But that's the big difference between Larry and Palmerston. Palmerston would have killed that pigeon. He's more bloodthirsty.

Even if Larry's food doesn't always come from his kills, at least the taxpayer can rest easy knowing that the chief mouser hasn't cost voters a penny. 'We came together as a group of staff and put some money in to start things off,' says Sugg. 'We had an annual Larry quiz around Christmas, a fundraiser to pay for all of his food. We had Secretaries of State come and do quiz rounds. The Prime Minister came up and did one. I think most rounds were cat-related: famous cats of the world, cats in history…'

In September 2016, the bill for Larry's vet care two months earlier was brought up in the House of Lords in a written question to the Cabinet Office from Lord Blencathra. In her reply, government whip Baroness Chisholm of Owlpen was the first to refer to Larry as chief mouser in the parliamentary record: 'The costs were met through voluntary staff donations due to their affection for Larry. There was no compulsion to donate and no refunds have been requested. The remaining funds will contribute towards the future upkeep of the Chief Mouser.'

Clearly, Larry brought much joy to the Downing Street staff. Working in politics can be extremely stressful – especially in an important, high-stakes job such as Sugg's, which required her to be constantly at the Prime Minister's side, whether at home or abroad. 'I used to go and give Larry a little stroke when things were all getting a bit much. I think everybody did. He's very much a street cat, he can look after himself. He's never going to be a lap cat, but you could pick him up and give him a stroke,' she says.

One of Sugg's favourite moments of her six years at Downing Street was the street party held in April 2011, the day of the wedding of Prince William and Kate Middleton.

> I remember making a bow tie for Larry. I just took a little Union Jack napkin from the street party we were holding in Downing Street, folded it up and taped it on his collar. And then we took a photo – at that stage he liked walking up and down the Cabinet Room table, so it was taken there. Little did I know it would be used around the world!

But some people liked Larry a bit too much: 'Larry did get a bit overweight. There was an email sent around saying, "Larry is very well fed and very well looked-after – so if he's coming to you looking hungry, he's not."'

Larry at one stage also had a little friend called Maisie, a cat who visited him from across the road at St James's Park. She belonged to the park keeper and lived in a cottage there. Before Larry came to Downing Street, Battersea did what every responsible cat owner should do and neutered Larry, so any relationship with Maisie was only ever going to be platonic.

Relations were often less harmonious with the other Whitehall cats, particularly with Palmerston at the Foreign Office, next door to Downing Street. 'Larry can hold his own. He's a street-fighting cat from Wandsworth. Most of the cats stayed away. And if they ever dared come into his zone, he sent them packing,' says Sugg.

'Cats are territorial, of course, so guarding his territory was a natural reaction,' says Haddon.

> All that yowling that took place was also natural behaviour. Aggression between cats often starts with staring, then moves on to loud yowling, and only after that is there a fight. Larry must have had a fairly bold temperament to fight Palmerston when he strayed into his turf.
>
> My recommendation, when he and Palmerston kept fighting, was that they should have made sure Larry had places to sit high up at the front of Downing Street – like a few ledges he could sit on and survey whether Palmerston was in the neighbourhood. Or maybe an outdoor cat tree somewhere near the front door. It would have meant that Larry could know in advance when Palmerston was nearby, rather than just running into him.

In 2020, Larry bested a fox in Downing Street, chasing it away, and, while not the streetfighter some thought he would be, he can be feisty at times.

Ng has been chronicling those fights and Larry's other adventures with his camera for some time. And while he has taken some dramatic action shots, the Australian tells *Political Animals* that the No. 10 cat can be very calm too.

> The thing I first noticed about Larry was just how nonchalant

> he was. He would just not care about anything that was going on. I remember one time he was just sleeping in the middle of the street while we were waiting for a political leader to turn up to see the Prime Minister. And he just didn't have a care in the world. It's funny, because it can be quite a stressful street, as you know. People are often jostling for position to see what's going to happen. But he's a real contrast to that, isn't he? I guess he feels that it's his domain, so he just does whatever he feels like. We just work around him!

Ng feels he has become good friends with Larry, and he has shared many stories about the Downing Street cats with his social media followers over the years.

> Larry and Palmerston have very different personalities. Palmerston is the younger cat and more aggressive and outgoing. Larry is more like an elder statesman. He's more reserved, I would say, kind of like a beautiful Englishman. But when he gets to know you, he will then open up and be a bit friendlier. There are stories about Larry being standoffish with a lot of people. And it's true. If you're a stranger and he doesn't know you, then he's going to be very defensive.

One way to gain Larry's trust – and his friendship? You guessed it: Dreamies.

> There was a point where he was put on a diet, and I was very specifically told, 'You are not allowed to feed the cat.' Larry had put on half a kilo in weight. So he was stopped from

having Dreamies. The only thing I feed him these days is wet box sticks. They're a bit healthier for him, but they do give him bad breath!

Many of Ng's photos of Larry have gone around the world, some of them helped by the @Number10cat Twitter account. The 'Larry the Cat' account styles itself as the true voice of the 'Chief Mouser to the Cabinet Office. 18 year old tabby. Living with my sixth Prime Minister. Unofficial. I am the media, miaow'. The account was set up in February 2011 and has some 868,000 followers at the time of writing. Ng's own Twitter following of some 32,000 has been boosted by his photos of the King of Downing Street, too:

> Japan, Brunei, Malaysia, Singapore, the Bahamas… people all over the world have seen the photos. I did some merchandising too. I wanted to just exercise my creativity because there was no kind of market for this stuff. But now there's about a million copycats. I did some tote bags initially, because I had this photograph of him sleeping in the middle of the road and the phrase on it was: 'When sleeping on a job is the job.'
>
> I think Larry's appeal is the fact that he's so nonchalant. I still remember when Trump came to meet Theresa May, Larry was sleeping on the windowsill on the left, and so I had to go shoot a lot wider to get him in. At one point, he was just licking his bits before Trump was about to show up!

In his first UK interview, the author of the @Number10cat account, who wishes to remain anonymous, tells *Political Animals*:

As soon as I saw that Cameron had installed a new chief mouser I thought it would be fun for people to hear what he had to say. Bringing in Larry was obviously something of a PR exercise for the government, but they didn't think to claim a social media presence. I'm sure they would now.

On the day Larry arrived, a few different accounts appeared – two ultimately stuck around. Mine and @downingstreetcat. Mine was always a little more politically focused, but the key thing was engaging with people. Social media should be social. In those early days Larry replied to everyone. I still would, if there weren't so many messages.

The content is certainly more political now, and generally fairly disparaging of the government of the day.

I recognise that it's changed over the years, though I genuinely feel the content has ultimately centred on three things: politics, cats and humour – and the best posts encompass all three. One of my favourite early ones was a Tory health minister asking Larry why CAT scans were so expensive and Larry having to explain that they weren't performed by actual cats… proof that the humour of the account has always been ropey!

The account's more political bent has left some in Westminster feeling it has veered too much from its original purpose of tweets about Larry.

It's fair to say that the account has been increasingly critical [of those in power] – I think part of that was down to the handling of the pandemic and the subsequent revelations and scandals. People were rightly angry and I think it's natural that Larry, witness to the events, reflected some of that anger.

The account would still work if it was just Larry and cat content, but I think adding politics into the mix is apt and has helped it to reach a wider audience. Obviously it also means it's not for some people, and that's entirely fair enough – there are plenty of accounts dedicated to cats being cute for them to enjoy!

The reaction to the account is what's kept it going for so long. Lots of people seem to like hearing from Larry. I've said before that the UK is a nation of animal lovers, and so it needs a national animal to love. Larry is that animal and the account hopefully celebrates that.

One of the most popular types of post has always been sharing the work of the photographers who work on Downing Street. They've all been very kind in letting me share images of Larry, and I've always ensured they get credit, which has helped them to build their audiences.

Right from the start I thought it was best to remain anonymous for the account to work properly. Some people run accounts like this and put their details in the bio, which always feels a bit of a shame. Obviously people don't think they're talking to an actual cat, but it's fun to pretend. I'll miss Larry when he's gone, and at least a few people on social media will too.

Larry's appeal is clear, and not just online. An exclusive poll for *Political Animals* by Deltapoll suggests that 47 per cent of the British public has heard of Larry, far more than any of the other political animals of Westminster featured in this book. The number rises to 58 per cent of people aged 55–64 and 61 per cent of people over 65 – he's a popular cat with older people.

What both Ng and Larry's anonymous Twitter alter ego know well is that Larry has global fame and love. Sometimes this has come from unexpected places, such as Barack Obama's 'body man', Marvin Nicholson. Arriving ahead of the President's trip to Downing Street in May 2011, Nicholson specifically asked to see Larry. 'Marvin was just obsessed with Larry, unbeknownst to me,' remembers Sugg.

> His colleagues told me he even had Larry on his screensaver in his office in the White House. So I took him down to see Larry, who I think was in the garden room at the time. Marvin was delighted to meet him and took loads of photos. Then he says, 'We've got to introduce him to the President.' And I said, 'Really?' And when I told the Prime Minister, he said, 'Really?'

Part of the President's visit involved a barbecue in the Downing Street garden, with Obama and Cameron flipping burgers and sizzling hot dogs for the servicemen and women attending the event.

> They went outside, did the barbecue and then on the way back in, Marvin said, 'Right, now is the time. Where's Larry? We've got to introduce Larry to the President.'
>
> So I went off and got Larry. He doesn't love being held … The Prime Minister and the President came through and Marvin introduced Obama to Larry. So Larry met the President, but I just remember holding him tightly to make sure he

didn't do anything like scratch the President – we were surrounded by Secret Service agents – and being covered head to waist in cat fur because Larry had been making his feelings known about hanging around waiting.

The President said to me, 'You are covered in cat fur.' And I said, 'Yes, Mr President, yes, I am.' So that's why I probably look a bit uncomfortable in the photo!

The photo, reproduced in this book, went around the world: Sugg, a Prime Minister, a President and a globally famous cat. Obama later presented Larry with a toy rat on behalf of the American people, which Larry approved of.

The presidential meeting is not the only example of Larry's mere presence making a photo or piece of footage worthy of note. He made a splash in 2018 just by slipping into No. 10. A Sky News reporter was broadcasting about a recent Brexit controversy and the finance bill while Larry was sat outside the Downing Street door waiting to be let in. As the door is bomb-proof, there is no cat flap. Indeed, the whole street has been gated off since an IRA terrorist attack against Prime Minister John Major in February 1991; these days, access is only permitted to authorised visitors. As Larry waited, the duty policeman knocked on the door, it was opened and in sauntered Larry. The clip went viral, though the Sky News reporter's discussion of the Brexit finance bill is long forgotten.

In 2019, his image was used in a mocked-up photograph by the *Daily Mail*, which 'reported' as an April Fool's Day joke that Larry was going to get a cat flap in the door of No. 10. At the height of the Brexit debate, the paper wrote:

After all the pussyfooting about how to leave, it seems life has just become a lot easier for one occupant of No 10. Not Theresa May – but Larry the Downing Street cat. Our pictures show a cat flap that mysteriously appeared overnight in the building's famous front door. Larry was recruited as chief mouser to the Cabinet Office in 2011 but has always had to wait for a human to open the door.

Larry has also been known to get in the way. As Theresa May was about to make her resignation speech outside No. 10 in 2019, Larry had to be removed by a member of staff so as not to distract from May's statement, prompting loud boos from the assembled press pack. When I've been reporting from Downing Street and seen Larry whisked away on other occasions, for example when a dignitary was about to arrive, I may even have joined the chorus of boos myself.

Two years after his presidential encounter, Larry was to meet five more global superstars. This time it was a group of young men who number amongst the few people to have been screamed at by excited fans as much as if not more than Barack Obama: One Direction. In 2013, the boyband came to No. 10 to film a charity single for Comic Relief. But the main attraction of their visit was not the Prime Minister. 'That was a big day for Downing Street,' Sugg recalls.

> We had to try to encourage people to get on with their work, rather than just happen to be wandering past to meet One Direction. They were upstairs using the Thatcher study as their green room. I think it was Louis Tomlinson who said, 'Where's

Larry? Is he around?' So I went and got Larry and introduced him to all the boys – his fame even went as far as One Direction.

Nicole Scherzinger came to switch the Christmas lights on in 2012. At one point she was asking about the cat. At all the charity functions we used to try to get him there, whether out in the garden or up in the state rooms, because everyone always loved seeing him.

Strangely, rumours grew of tensions between Cameron and Larry. To Sugg and others in Downing Street, 'it became a weird thing that the Prime Minister "didn't like" Larry' because it was 'very far from the truth'. One story alleged that Cameron didn't like his suits getting covered with Larry's cat hair. The *Daily Telegraph* reported that Cameron disparagingly referred to Larry as 'it' in conversations. Public opinion, inasmuch as social media is any guide of that, supported Larry, but the rumours persisted until Cameron left office on 13 July 2016 after losing the Brexit referendum. But Larry was to remain (though perhaps after asking to be let out and then in again).

Cameron confronted the issue of his relationship with Larry head on in his final Prime Minister's Questions. Addressing MPs in the House of Commons, Cameron took

> the opportunity to put a rumour to rest ... it is even more serious than the *Strictly Come Dancing* one. The Right Honourable Gentleman [Jeremy Corbyn, then opposition leader] will appreciate this because El Gato, his cat, is particularly famous. This is the rumour that somehow I do not love Larry; I do, and I have photographic evidence to prove it.

Cameron then brandished a photo of Larry sitting on his lap in his office, taken by Sugg that morning. She remembers: 'Larry used to come into the PM's office quite regularly, particularly around Prime Minister's Questions prep sessions. He was sitting there, stroking Larry on his lap, saying, "I can't believe people don't think I like Larry." So I took a photo.' In the House of Commons, Cameron continued: 'Sadly, I cannot take Larry with me. He belongs to the house, and the staff love him very much, as do I.'

More photos were taken that morning but have never been shared beyond the small team helping him prepare for his Commons grilling – until now. The former Prime Minister has kindly given permission for one of these to be published in *Political Animals*. It is a playful photo of Cameron leaning his head down beside Larry, taken just before Cameron headed to PMQs and then on to Buckingham Palace to see Queen Elizabeth II and resign as Prime Minister. Like the photo that was shown to the House of Commons, it was taken by Sugg, loyal to both Cameron and Larry to the final day, and beyond.

Theresa May, the incoming Prime Minister, was more of a dog person, though she didn't have any pets herself. However, it was clear Larry was going nowhere. Sugg even offered to rehome Larry and act as his guardian should the May administration not want him. But they did, as has every administration since. To ensure Larry is only looked after by people who want him, Sugg has made the offer each time an administration has changed since she left Downing Street alongside Cameron. She was always, she says, 'very careful to make sure that Larry was the whole house's cat'.

When I look back, I'm very proud of many things we did in six and a half years in Downing Street. It's been a while since then and a lot has happened – sometimes it's hard to come up with a long list of those things that have endured, but Larry is definitely on that. And he's still at No. 10, regardless of the multiple changes in Prime Minister. I think all the PMs understood Larry was a permanent fixture – unlike them.

With the 2017 general election looming, *The Guardian* imagined how Larry might be feeling about the potential arrival of Jeremy Corbyn and El Gato. Written from Larry's perspective, the article said: 'My real worry is what happens if May calls an early election and Jezza wins. I hear he has a feline called El Gato and I really don't fancy sharing this gaff. I didn't vote to leave the EU only to end up with a Spanish housemate.'

Larry turned eighteen in 2025, which is a good age for a male cat. Downing Street staff I spoke to for *Political Animals* have noticed his advancing years, of course, as have observers outside the black door. 'He's certainly getting thinner,' says Ng. 'As all cats age, they do lose weight. But he's still coming to get me for snacks. Every time he sees me, he comes straight over. He will lead me to my bag and those treats.'

Some people get more bad-tempered as they age, but a number of politicians maintain that Larry has long been this way. Boris Johnson called him a 'thug' who 'mauled' his dog Dilyn, who had tried to steal Larry's food. Speaking to *Political Animals*, Johnson elaborates: 'I don't think Larry is one of those cats who comes forward to be nuzzled and petted; I don't remember that. I liked Larry, but he was pretty fierce and territorial.'

Ian Murray, Scotland Secretary under Sir Keir Starmer, had even nastier things to say about Larry when he spoke to business leaders in Glasgow in September 2024. He recounted how many new Cabinet members had been looking forward to getting photos with Larry, but he was not playing ball. 'Without putting too fine a point on it, Larry the cat is a little s***,' summarised Murray. 'So none of us got a picture with Larry the cat. Larry the cat is the most miserable animal you'll ever meet in your life. I'm not surprised, given who he's had to live with for the last ten years.'

One Westminster insider has a different take: 'Let's have a look at the evidence here. Boris doesn't like him. He refused a stroke from Liz Truss. He refused a photo with Ian Murray. Perhaps Larry is just a good judge of character?'

The perennial question remains for some: is Larry just a bit of a curmudgeon? And how has he changed over the years? Sugg admits that he's got a bit grumpy:

> But to be fair, he's never been ungrumpy. He's got attitude. Cattitude. He's seen people in and he's seen people out. He is an institution. He's improved the mental health of the staff who work at the building and been a welcome distraction when things get a little stressful.
>
> He's also a very British cat. He's done Downing Street proud. He captured everybody's hearts.

Speaking of her time in No. 10, Sonia Khan, who has also volunteered at Battersea Dogs & Cats Home, agrees with this analysis.

> I got a lot of one-to-one time with Larry, who is the most

fawned over but also the most ambivalent cat I've ever met. I say this as someone who has a dog but has a son who loves cats: I've never met a cat that is much more independent and totally unbothered by his profile. He embodies the best of Britain. He is a cult icon.

Larry, sadly, will not live for ever. When Her Majesty Queen Elizabeth II died, there was a long-standing plan for her funeral arrangements. The phrase 'London Bridge has fallen' was used to alert police officers that the monarch had passed. Similar operations are in place, we are told, for when Larry sadly crosses the rainbow bridge. *The Times* reported in August 2024 that a plan jokingly entitled 'Larry Bridges' is on the stocks at Downing Street.

Larry's legacy will be a long one, for many reasons. He's even immortalised on Google Street View as, by chance, Larry was having a snooze outside the black door when Google took their shots of Downing Street in June 2012.

At the time of writing, however, Larry is still around and thriving. He even has some new housemates in Sir Keir Starmer's cats Jojo and Prince, although they are kept well apart from Larry.

One Downing Street insider who has known Larry since he came to live in the house revealed that Larry still gets many gifts and toys from the public, although he isn't given any food sent, in case it has been tampered with. 'He still gets paintings, pictures, letters from children of course, but also animal lovers in general,' says the insider. 'The Direct Communication Unit at No. 10 deal with all his post. He is fed by a select group of people, a cleaner from the domestic staff, the custodians [security staff], messengers and "front of house" staff – that's only because most of those staff are working shifts around the clock.'

With such a long tenure in Downing Street, far longer than the Prime Ministers, many of the civil servants and almost all the special advisers, Larry is content and is impressed by very little, knowing as he does that all is well as long as his will is obeyed. 'Larry takes everything in his stride and knows exactly who's boss. He will let you know very quickly when he's had enough!' says the long-time insider.

They also note that Larry doesn't go far from No. 10; he knows where his friends – and the radiators – are:

> These days, he mostly hangs out at the front door, the front hall above the radiators, near the ground-floor lift lobby in Downing Street. He can also be found across the road at the Foreign Office or in the police boxes. He's known to spend time in a police box with a police officer, both keeping warm and for company. He also spends time at the Cabinet Office nature area at the back of the Cabinet Office on Downing Street, where the foxes hang out. He does his business there as it's quiet and secluded.

As is natural for a male cat of his age, there is always concern for his wellbeing. 'His health is good, but he is old now and has regular visits from the vet just as a formal check-up from time to time,' says the insider. 'Larry specifically eats wet food and has cat milk as a treat now he's getting on. He is much loved by all staff and has been during all the time he has been at Downing Street and I hope he is here for many years to come.'

Larry has remained loyal to his origins at Battersea Dogs & Cats Home by supporting them on Twitter. On International Cat Day, he posted about their drive for cats to be microchipped. As junior minister in the Department for Environment, Food and Rural Affairs Robbie Moore MP told the House of Commons in April 2024:

> Since we introduced the English compulsory cat microchipping legislation, we have been working closely with a number of animal welfare stakeholders to develop a coordinated communications campaign to explain to cat owners the benefits of microchipping and the new legal requirements.
>
> Last summer, we even enlisted the support of our chief mouser, Larry the cat, who himself was once an un-microchipped stray before being taken in and rehomed by Battersea Dogs & Cats Home. Larry's tweet on International Cat Day, explaining the importance of microchipping for reuniting pets with their owners, received half a million impressions.

Battersea's head of catteries and feline welfare, Lindsey Quinlan, says:

> It seems like only yesterday that Larry came to our cattery as a stray in need of a home. I don't think anyone back then could have imagined just how incredible his life would turn out to be.

At Battersea, we work hard to ensure that every animal goes to their ideal home, whether that be a cottage in the country or the most famous street in the UK. While the majority of our cats are content with a comfy sofa, some cats such as Larry prefer to 'work' for their supper – from keeping an eye out for pests on a farm to entertaining the political press with their pigeon-chasing antics.

Sugg, Larry's original cat mum, believes his appeal is enduring for clear reasons. 'Given cats are such a popular pet in the UK, I think people can associate their cats with Larry and like the fact that he's in Downing Street,' she says.

I also think Larry kind of humanises the office of Prime Minister. It's a nice, optimistic thing. Hopefully, no one's going to hate Larry. It cut through some of the difficulties around politics, and I think people feel quite affectionate towards him; they feel like he represents the country, in a way.

Just as Larry has shown loyalty to Battersea, so too has he shown loyalty to his friends who were instrumental in bringing him to Downing Street. Gary O'Donoghue now works in Washington DC as the BBC's chief North America correspondent. Helping out back in London on the BBC's 2024 general election coverage, he found himself back on his old Downing Street beat. 'I think it was the Saturday, two days after the election,' recalls O'Donoghue. 'It was during the England game against Switzerland in Euro 2024. It was quiet between broadcasts and we were hanging around watching the football and Larry came over.'

Sugg was elevated by Cameron to the House of Lords, where she sits on the Conservative benches as Baroness Sugg. There, she speaks mainly on issues of international development, gender equality, sexual and reproductive health and education. She was also made a minister by Theresa May in the Department for International Development and then the Foreign, Commonwealth and Development Office. However, when Rishi Sunak, as Chancellor under Johnson, announced in 2020 that the foreign aid budget was to be cut, Sugg resigned in protest.

> I was very sad about it and I didn't want to go, but I felt I had no option. I handed in my resignation and said my goodbyes to everyone at the Foreign Office. As I left the building, Larry walked across Downing Street into the Foreign Office quad and came towards me. I hadn't seen him there before, and while of course I know he's a cat and so wasn't aware what was going on, it was an emotional day so I hope I can be forgiven for thinking he had come to say goodbye to me. I gave him a stroke and took one last photo of the two of us. It was a nice moment on a difficult day.

Larry – loyal to the end.

CHAPTER TWELVE

ONE PRIME MINISTER ON HIS DOG: BORIS JOHNSON ON DILYN

Dilyn the Jack Russell's three years in Downing Street were almost as eventful as Boris Johnson's.

Born in 2018 with a misaligned jaw, Dilyn was going to be put down by the breeder as he could not be sold. Sadly this type of heartlessness is typical of some breeders, particularly unlicensed ones. Thankfully, he was taken in by Friends of Animals Wales and was adopted in 2019 by Johnson and his then partner (now wife) Carrie Symonds. 'Dilyn' means 'follow' in Welsh and he was given the name as a tribute to a recently deceased spaniel who had been cared for by the shelter.

Carrie Johnson is clearly devoted to Dilyn, notably defending her dog in a clash with Johnson's chief adviser Dominic Cummings in a row which some say had long-term consequences for the administration. In May 2021, Cummings alleged that the Prime Minister was slower in his Covid response than he could have been because on the morning he had to decide his pandemic strategy, there were two distractions: one was Donald Trump talking about bombing Iraq; the other concerned Dilyn. An article in *The Times* suggested Dilyn was going to be rehomed because his training was not going well.

Symonds tweeted that the report was 'a load of total crap.

There has never been a happier, healthier and more loved dog than our Dilyn. 100 per cent bs. The people behind this story should be ashamed of themselves'. According to Cummings, Symonds demanded that the press office deal with the story. In evidence to Parliament at a later inquiry, Cummings said:

> It sounds so surreal it couldn't possibly be true ... We had this completely insane situation in which part of the building was saying, 'Are we going to bomb Iraq?', part of the building was arguing about whether or not we were going to do quarantine ... and the Prime Minister has his girlfriend going crackers about something completely trivial.

Cummings left Downing Street in November 2020 – nine months after he sacked me as a special adviser. By the time he resigned, the battles between Cummings and Symonds had become too much. She had won.

There were also allegations that Cummings disliked Dilyn for another reason: his habit of humping. As Boris Johnson explains to *Political Animals*:

> Dilyn is really quite an affectionate dog, very affectionate. And he made strong amorous advances on Cummings. At one point, he really kept rogering his leg in a pretty sort of thoroughgoing way. Poor old Cummings went absolutely purple with excitement as this was going on. I had to pull Dilyn off. After a while.
>
> Dilyn's pretty indiscriminate. Pretty much anybody was the object of his affection.

Dilyn was eventually neutered in 2021, having displayed his romantic nature perhaps a little too often.

Reflecting on this behaviour, Celia Haddon observes that

> Jack Russells are very energetic dogs. They are not always suited to town life. Public schools in Victorian times felt that boys should work out their animal spirits on the playing fields. So if Dilyn was only taken for a short daily walk in the No. 10 garden, that may have meant he had an excess of energy. Or maybe he humped to get attention. 'Get down' *is* attention.
>
> Humping can be a form of stress relief for dogs, so possibly he found life in No. 10 with babies etc. stressful. They have strong hunting instincts and are not the easiest dogs to train.
>
> Boris and Carrie, though, should be congratulated for getting a rescue dog, not buying an expensive pedigree. It was a kind act.

Dilyn became well known for his bad behaviour, particularly at Chequers, the Prime Minister's country residence. A Downing Street insider tells me how he once had to wait awkwardly during a meeting there while Boris removed a deposit of Dilyn's dried faeces from under the table. 'It was clear it had been there for some time,' says the insider.

On another occasion, Dilyn darted under Johnson's feet, clutching an old book in his jaws. The Prime Minister reportedly shouted, 'For God's sake, I'm going to get another £1,000 repair bill! Someone please shoot that f****** dog!'

Katie Lam, now an MP, was a special adviser to Johnson at No. 10 and the lucky recipient of another of Dilyn's 'presents'.

Johnson waves off the incident, however: 'I don't think he defecated in Katie Lam's handbag. Was the charge urination? I mean, what's a spot of urine between friends? In my experience, girls have all sorts of things in their handbags.'

But Dilyn's high jinks were a far cry from his grim start in life, before he arrived at Friends of Animals Wales, run by Eileen Jones. Introducing Dilyn on Twitter, Symonds tweeted, 'Thanks to the wonderful Eileen who rescued Dilyn after she got a tip-off that he was to be dumped by a puppy dealer because he was born with a crooked jaw. Eileen fixed his little jaw and saved his life. She is a hero.'

The Johnsons were introduced to Friends of Animals Wales by TV vet Marc Abraham. He later commented that 'Carrie and Boris are helping a very, very vulnerable dog that's otherwise likely to be killed'. When Dilyn arrived at Downing Street, a spokesman said, 'The PM has always been a passionate supporter of animal welfare and believes in giving animals the best start in life.'

Jones added at the time:

> It's a wonderful rags-to-riches story, but for such a small dog, he has a huge amount on his shoulders. His adoption raises awareness of the campaign against puppy farming and also highlights the importance of adopting, rather than shopping for puppies.
>
> It's great that Carrie and Boris have picked such a normal, scruffy little terrier rather than some designer pooch. He's had a great start, he was well-looked after and has taken his favourite toys and bed. He's a real little character and I'm sure he's going to settle in.

Dilyn's big public moment came when he accompanied Johnson to his local polling station on election day in 2019, wearing a blue sash. Dilyn had also followed Carrie around the country during the campaign as she supported various candidates, including Zac Goldsmith in Richmond Park in south-west London. Goldsmith shared a photograph of himself holding Dilyn and another dog, Pepper, in his arms, writing, 'Thank you to Pepper and Dilyn for your support today – you were both excellent on the doorstep.'

On polling day, the hashtag #DogsAtPollingStations trended, as it has in many elections in recent years. When news of the eighty-seat Conservative victory came through, many papers around the world carried pictures of Johnson and Dilyn together. The *New York Post*'s headline was 'Conservatives Lick Labour', accompanied by a photo of Dilyn with his tongue out.

In contrast, the Labour leader at the time, Jeremy Corbyn, made clear his cat would not be accompanying him to his local polling station in Islington, north London, having previously stated El Gato was perhaps 'a bit of a Tory' as he displayed 'disappointing individualism and a lack of concern for others'. In January 2025, Corbyn tweeted: 'It is with great sadness that I have to announce that El Gato died on Sunday. He gave joy to many throughout his life. He was happy, gentle and full of personality. Life will not be the same without El Gato's company and friendship.'

Dilyn loomed large in Downing Street as Johnson dealt with weighty matters of state, including how to respond to coronavirus. In his book *Pandemic Diaries*, Matt Hancock, who was Health Secretary for most of the pandemic, claims that Johnson once asked chief medical officer Professor Chris Whitty to test

Dilyn for Covid, as the dog had been wheezing and was short of breath.

> There was a long, awkward pause while [chief scientist] Patrick Vallance and the Prof tried to work out whether he was joking or whether we needed to summon the chief vet to provide a considered response. Eventually the Prof broke the silence. 'I don't know if the human antibody test would be suitable.'

Relations between Dilyn and Larry were, of course, always going to be subject to speculation. Johnson tells *Political Animals* it was clear Dilyn was scared of the cat right from the start of his time in Downing Street:

> Larry very jealously guarded his territory, I can tell you. And much against the advice of my private office, but with the overwhelming support of all the other officials in Downing Street, I decided I wanted to get a dog, so we got Dilyn.
>
> He's the sweetest little dog you could imagine, but he had a slightly misshapen jaw, which is actually one of the reasons why he never bites people. Poor little guy: he was going to be put down at birth. He is an absolutely sweet dog, but he made a mistake very early on of working out where Larry's food was, which was in one of the offices on the right of No. 10 as you go in. And there was a bowl of fishy stuff that Larry ate. And one day Dilyn went in and snaffled it. After that they developed the most incredible feud between them.
>
> I don't know if you've actually interviewed Larry for this

book, but Larry is entirely pyramidical in structure; he's built like a sumo wrestler and shaped like a Dorito. He's very, very heavy and strong and he scratched the life out of poor Dilyn.

And after that, Dil Dil just wouldn't go anywhere near him. He would flatten himself on the carpet and wouldn't move. And I would have to pick him up and carry him because he was so terrified. I think he has a very healthy respect for that cat.

Johnson expanded on this theme in one of his columns for the *Daily Mail*:

Have you ever reached out idly in a pub to take a chip from someone else's plate, and found yourself unexpectedly stabbed in the hand by a fork? That is the kind of reaction that Dilyn provoked from the Downing Street mouser.

The poor dog was quite badly mauled.

If legions of Larry fans are shocked by this portrait of the famous feline – well, I think the public have a right to know the truth.

Johnson also referenced Dilyn's strained working relationship with Larry in his final speech on the steps of No. 10 in July 2022: 'If Dilyn and Larry can put behind them their occasional difficulties then so can the Conservative Party.'

Alas, Dilyn and Queen Elizabeth II's swans were another match perhaps not made in heaven. In *Charles III: New King. New Court. The Inside Story*, royal biographer Robert Hardman explained that as Johnson recovered from Covid in 2020, the Queen generously made the grounds of Buckingham Palace available so the Prime

Minister could walk privately and build up his lung capacity. Against the advice of aides, Johnson brought Dilyn with him. During one of these walks, Dilyn allegedly attacked a gosling. 'At their next encounter,' Hardman writes, 'the Queen nonchalantly talked about walking in the palace gardens before adding crisply: "I gather Jack Russells don't go very well with goslings."'

When Boris and Carrie Johnson left Downing Street in 2022, his successor Liz Truss complained of fleas in the No. 11 apartment, which left her and her family scratching. 'The entire place had to be sprayed with flea killer,' she wrote in her memoir *Ten Years to Save the West*. Sir Jeremy Hunt, who moved into the No. 11 flat as Chancellor after Truss's forty-nine days as Prime Minister, experienced the same issue. He replaced all the carpets, which were purchased at 'my own expense – vast expense because it had to be a security-cleared company that did it', he said during a speech in Washington DC.

But Dilyn had many fans. The Kennel Club reported that the popularity of Jack Russells increased by 30 per cent between 2018 and 2019. Club spokesman Bill Lambert noted:

> High-profile owners and popular culture can have a huge impact on the popularity of certain breeds, though we'd urge people to always do their research rather than follow a trend. The Jack Russell, for example, has certainly seen a surge of interest since Dilyn first put his paws through the door of Downing Street.

In December 2020, Dilyn appeared on the official No. 10 Christmas card draped in tinsel.

And it turns out Dilyn may have inadvertently acquired some political skills of his own, according to Johnson in his interview for *Political Animals*:

> Dilyn was a highly effective ice breaker. He was a genius diplomat. I had to do a complicated deal with a very nice Indian zillionaire called Bharti Mittal to buy a load of satellites in the days when I thought the UK would be competing with Elon [Musk], because low Earth orbit satellites are obviously where it was going to be.
>
> And we did this fantastic deal. We got these satellites, but Dilyn was instrumental, because he managed to get hold of Bharti Mittal's spectacles case and chew it enthusiastically. After that, all Bharti Mittal's commercial defences were down, and we did a very good deal.
>
> Dilyn is worth his weight in gold millions of times over.

CHAPTER THIRTEEN

ONE PRIME MINISTER ON HIS CATS: SIR KEIR STARMER ON JOJO AND PRINCE

Part of the inspiration for writing this book came in 2024, when I spoke to a senior source deep inside Sir Keir Starmer's leadership team about a crucial matter: what would happen to Jojo, the Starmer family cat, if Labour won the general election, as all the polls predicted? Would Jojo stay in the Starmers' constituency home in north London or come with the family to Downing Street?

My source was unequivocal: Jojo would be coming to No. 10. But when? It takes a few days for families to fully move into Downing Street, especially when the new Prime Minister has so many other priorities. The Starmers would be moving not into the smaller No. 10 flat, but the larger No. 11 flat, so Jojo would have plenty of room.

Four days after the July 2024 general election, a separate senior source who, like her boss, had moved from opposition to government, confirmed to me that Jojo had safely moved into his new home in Downing Street and was settling in nicely. When I posted this kitty exclusive on my Twitter account, @petercardwell, the reaction was instant and global. Retweets and comments came from the UK, the USA and even as far away as Japan and Colombia. It was seen by more than one and a half million people.

Since he arrived in July 2024, Jojo has been kept separate from No. 10's long-term resident Larry; in fact the two haven't even met. Given how territorial Larry has become, it was thought best to keep the two tomcats away from one another, with Jojo in the 11 Downing Street flat and Larry in his usual domain of the main hallway and environs of No. 10.

'Jojo is a long-standing Starmer cat, and he's fantastic,' Prime Minister Sir Keir Starmer tells *Political Animals*. 'He's particularly good at catching mice, which, when you're in Downing Street, is a very good attribute. He's merciless with them. And so I think the message goes around in the mouse world that ours is not a flat to pop up in.'

Jojo, a domestic shorthair who is about nine years old, is a rescue from a shelter in south London. The Starmers have had him for around eight years at the time of writing. And when he moved to Downing Street, he was not the only cat in the No. 11 flat for long. In September 2024, Sir Keir announced he had purchased Prince, a Siberian kitten, to join Jojo. After a summer of lobbying from their teenage daughter, the Starmers decided the time had come for a second cat. The Prime Minister says that Jojo has 'acclimatised' to his new, younger kitty brother.

> Our daughter negotiated a kitten, and obviously for Jojo as the established cat, that was a bit of a challenge to start with, but they are getting on all right now. The kitten, every now and again, does a sort of kamikaze jump off furniture onto the back of Jojo, which can be quite amusing for everyone – apart from Jojo!

Clearly Jojo and Prince are getting on well, but what about the Prime Minister's relationship with the top cat at Downing Street?

> Larry's on the door when I come in and out, and so it's always good to see him there. He gets more attention than all the rest of us put together. I've had no end of international leaders where we do the handshake on the door but the moment Larry makes an appearance, their total focus goes somewhere else!

In June 2025, Starmer was at the G7 meeting of world leaders in Canada, leaving Angela Rayner, his deputy, in charge. When she got into her ministerial car to go to the House of Commons to stand in for Starmer at Prime Minister's Questions, disaster very nearly struck. As Rayner's ministerial Range Rover moved off, her driver nearly ran over Larry. It was only because of the journalists and photographers waiting on Downing Street shouting 'CAT!' to the driver that he slowed down. The clip went viral. So viral, in fact, that the Deputy Prime Minister herself WhatsApped it across the Atlantic to her boss.

'Angela had a close encounter!' Sir Keir tells *Political Animals*. 'I was at the G7 in Canada and Angela actually sent me the clip with a message saying: "All under control here, boss!"'

And it's not the first time Larry has been almost flattened by a politician's car on Downing Street. In 2019, he was resting under 'the Beast', President Trump's 9,000-kilo car. The vehicle carries bags of the President's blood type for medical emergencies, is hermetically sealed against chemical attacks and has doors eight inches thick and windows five inches thick. Not the kind of car a cat would survive being run over by. Larry was safely removed, having never really been at risk, but many newspapers commented on his choice of spot for a nap.

Starmer himself has always been an animal lover. Indeed, when he was a child his parents had a small donkey sanctuary. 'I was brought up in a rural home on the border of Surrey and Kent,' says the Prime Minister. 'We had four dogs for starters, but my mum and dad were always very fond of donkeys and rescued them. In the end, we had four donkeys in the back field, all of them rescue donkeys, which were very gentle animals.'

Starmer's mother, Josephine, suffered from Still's disease, a rare, incurable condition causing fevers, rashes and joint pain. In later life, she also lost the ability to speak, meaning she never had a conversation with Starmer's son and daughter, her grandchildren.

Josephine Starmer died just two weeks before Sir Keir was elected an MP in 2015. She had worked for many years as a nurse in hospital high-dependency units. Her rescue donkeys brought her much joy. 'My mum always struggled to walk, but the happiest times I've seen when she could walk was when she was walking with one of the donkeys alongside her,' says Starmer.

CHAPTER FOURTEEN

ONE FUTURE (?) PRIME MINISTER ON HIS DOGS: NIGEL FARAGE ON PEBBLE AND BAXTER

In May 2010, Nigel Farage nearly died when his plane, trailing a banner reading 'Vote UKIP', crashed in Northamptonshire. Amongst other injuries, two bones in his neck were crushed, leading to spinal problems that persist to this day. 'I have had total C5 and C6 [vertebrae] reconstruction,' he tells *Political Animals*. 'If I don't exercise and don't do the stretching, I will barely be able to walk. So it is very, very important to exercise.'

That exercise is helped by two very willing participants: the Reform UK leader's Labradors, Baxter and Pebble. 'Baxter, the elder dog, is just over five,' says Farage.

> We got him very shortly before lockdown happened, which meant I actually had time to go out and do more exercise than I'd probably done for many, many years.
>
> The younger dog, Pebble, she's just over two. They both come from a long line of gun dogs, so they're actually very easy dogs. They're both Labradors, both pedigrees. They're a breed that wants to please, so if you tell them off, they cower in the corner. They need a lot of exercise – they probably need a good two hours a day right now.
>
> I think having two is better than having one. They're friends

with each other, so you feel a bit less guilty when you go out for a couple of hours. They've got companionship and mostly get on very, very well. It's fun, you know, particularly when they start chasing each other and mock fighting.

Farage likes to take Baxter and Pebble out in the morning when he can, usually once during the week and at weekends, with other members of his family exercising the dogs on other days. 'I really like going out early when there's nobody about and walk through the woods,' he says. 'I thoroughly enjoy it. I chuck a ball and they collect it. We're on the coast, so sometimes they swim in the sea. It's almost like they've been here for ever. You literally can't imagine life without them, even when they annoy you.'

Pebble and Baxter have featured on election leaflets, including during the 2024 general election, when they were pictured alongside Farage in a very large Reform UK mail drop.

I've never, ever used my children politically – you would struggle to find any photograph of me with any one of my four kids. There was a picture of me and my grandson one Christmas Day, but then he was five months old and not that identifiable. I've always been very careful to keep family out of the public domain – once you put them in the public eye, they become fair game as well.

But I did do a party political broadcast with the dogs on a bench, sitting in a valley in Kent. If you put up doggy pictures on Facebook or Instagram, the number of likes you get is quite unbelievable.

Let's face it, we are very much a nation of dog lovers – we're very much a nation of animal lovers, much more than our neighbours in Europe. Clearly there's something about the English-speaking world's attitude towards animals that is different than in the Mediterranean south. Don't ask me what it is, but it's clearly there and it's clearly real.

Farage himself is immortalised in the form of a dog toy. Farage lovers – and indeed haters – can treat their pooch to a squeaky Nigel dog toy for a mere £17.99 from a company called Pet Hates Toys.

In April 2025, Farage pulled an April Fool's Day prank in which he was 'tattooed' with a British bulldog. In fact, it was a temporary tattoo from a studio in Cambridgeshire. Even when this was revealed as a joke, the animal rights group People for the Ethical Treatment of Animals (PETA) wrote to Farage urging him not to promote British bulldog imagery, as the breed tends to suffer from breathing difficulties. Reform UK responded by calling the group 'anti-British'.

But Farage himself is not just a dog man. 'I've had cats as well, some that almost turned feral living in the country. They can go off and fend for themselves very happily. I'm not against cats at all, but I just think it's a different relationship, isn't it? I mean a dog cannot survive without you.'

When *Political Animals* spoke to Farage in June 2025, a poll had just been released by Ipsos suggesting that Reform UK could have a majority in a forthcoming general election, meaning he could, hypothetically, become Prime Minister of the United Kingdom. So would Larry remain a fixture at No. 10 should Reform UK form the government?

'Of course! Larry is more important than any politician or Prime Minister,' says Farage. 'Let's get a sense of perspective here, please!'

PART V

THE POLITICAL ANIMALS OF PARLIAMENT

CHAPTER FIFTEEN

CRONUS THE TARANTULA

Being summoned to the Chief Whip's office is never something MPs relish. And that was particularly the case when they were aware that the most important political disciplinarian in the United Kingdom, a man who can make or break an MP's career, was accompanied by his pet tarantula.

The Chief Whip isn't the most high-profile or public role within the Cabinet, but it is one of the most important. He or she keeps the troops in order and will often recommend to the Prime Minister which MPs should be promoted, so they need to have their finger on the pulse of the parliamentary party. It is the role played by Ian Richardson in the original BBC drama *House of Cards*.

In 2017, after a disastrous general election for Theresa May, her Chief Whip Gavin Williamson was deeply involved with the confidence-and-supply agreement discussions with Northern Ireland's Democratic Unionist Party. By securing their backing for the May administration, a government could then be properly formed. It was a hard-fought deal by both sides and no small achievement of negotiation. But, Sir Gavin concedes, his role in that deal will be much further down the paragraphs of his obituary than his guardianship of Cronus, the eight-legged fiend who struck fear into the hearts of Conservative MPs. 'No one ever talks to me about pulling together the confidence-and-supply agreement with the DUP', Sir Gavin tells *Political Animals*. 'But I will virtually always get asked a question about Cronus. Cronus is the one people want to talk about!'

Cronus was purchased from Hollybush Garden Centre and Aquaria in Wolverhampton, in Sir Gavin's constituency. It was in 2014, two years before Williamson was elevated to the Cabinet, that Cronus came to live in the offices of her local MP. Male spiders live about five years, so, given that Cronus is still going strong at the time of writing – eleven years later – it's fair to assume that she is female. As Williamson didn't know Cronus's sex at the time of purchase, he decided a neutral name was the right option. 'I couldn't call it Bert, or, you know, Sharon. I suppose I should have called it Leslie/Lesley.'

In Greek mythology, Cronus was the leader of the first generation of the Titans. He overthrew his father, Uranus, by castrating him, and ruled during the Golden Age before being overthrown by his own son, Zeus, and imprisoned. While Sir Gavin did nothing nearly as drastic as that, there was perhaps an element of rebellion against his parents, who told him as a child that the spider he craved could not be his. 'Although I remember my grandmother saying to me, "Spiders are lucky,"' he recalls.

Sir Gavin is also keen to emphasise that Cronus pre-dates his time as Chief Whip.

> It was more that she came on the journey with me. I always loved arachnids but was never allowed to have one. My family don't come into my parliamentary office and are not keen on spiders. So I thought, I could perfectly happily have the spider I've always wanted here.

When I became Chief Whip, no one either noticed or was bothered for many, many months because I kept her in the office. I think it was the *Daily Telegraph* that broke the story. For a brief period, Cronus became the country's most famous arachnid.

I think it is the enduring affection and interest British people will always have about our pets. I appreciate that spiders are not quite the puppies people love – in fact, some people actively despise them – but there are those who absolutely love them.

So why spiders?

'It's just the genius of what spiders are able to do,' says Sir Gavin. 'They're amazingly clever creatures. Obviously, tarantulas don't capture their prey by webs. And I know they're incredibly clean animals. I mean, they sort of get rid of all the things that we don't want. They're a really fascinating creature that have a bit of a bad reputation.'

Unsurprisingly, some on the parliamentary estate didn't share Sir Gavin's enthusiasm for Cronus – or at least wanted to keep a healthy distance from her. Several Conservative MPs made it clear they didn't relish Cronus being part of proceedings.

> There were some colleagues who always wanted reassurance that the spider was either secure or had been removed from the room. There was one colleague who obviously had a deep fear of spiders. And before the meeting, we did sort of get a message to say, 'Is it possible if the spider isn't in the room?'

'A spider is not the cuddliest of companions,' admits Sir Gavin, who also has two cocker spaniels and a cat. And while Cronus has not yet featured on any election leaflets, his dogs have.

> I had a number of people say, 'Well, I don't like you, but I do like your dogs!' I think there is that sort of humanising side of it. If I was trying to have a PR blitz, on reflection, probably the spider isn't the sort of humanising creature that a PR adviser would suggest. When you were a special adviser, Peter, you wouldn't be putting it on the top of your list, for Mr Buckland to sit there stroking his arachnid on his hand as the Lord Chief Justice came to visit him.

And it wasn't just the spider Sir Gavin and his staff had to keep alive; it was the food for Cronus too. 'It's always good to have a supply of crickets,' he explains. 'You have to feed the food in order to keep that alive long enough for Cronus to be fed.'

While his dedicated staff did assist Sir Gavin with Cronus's welfare, he senses perhaps it would have been more appreciated had another animal been chosen.

> I think that they would really rather I had a cat or a dog. Maybe I'll have my cocker spaniel next to rebrand myself. I'm not so arrogant to think that I will ever be relaunched. But if you see me in my London office, cocker spaniel outside, you'll be like, 'What's he up to?'

CHAPTER SIXTEEN

ANIMALS IN PARLIAMENT

The best-known animals in the Houses of Parliament in recent years have been David Blunkett's succession of guide dogs. Blunkett had a successful career as leader of Sheffield Council for seven years before entering Parliament in 1987. Firstly Education and Employment Secretary, then Home Secretary and later Work and Pensions Secretary, Blunkett was a stalwart of the Blair years and has been a member of the House of Lords since 2015.

Blind since birth, Blunkett only got a guide dog as an adult, although his childhood home had an evolving menagerie of animals including white mice – his favourite was called Peterkin – rabbits, a tortoise and goldfish. He also had a male budgie called Bimbo who flew freely around the house. Blunkett remembers how looking after his rabbits at the boarding school he attended for blind children inspired his desire to take care of others as a politician.

Blunkett visited Parliament as a university student with his first guide dog, Ruby, in tow, but he was incensed when she was refused entry. With the help of the Guide Dogs for the Blind Association, who were campaigning at the time for universal access for guide dogs, Blunkett and Ruby's story made headlines in *The Guardian* and the *Mirror*. Later, in 1971, when the law had finally changed and he returned to Westminster as one of Sheffield's Labour councillors, Ruby became the first guide dog to be allowed into the Houses of Parliament. She was well-behaved on that occasion, but that was not always the case.

'Ruby was a wonderful dog and a diabolical guide dog,' Blunkett tells *Political Animals*. 'She was incredibly mischievous. She was able to take food off trolleys without stopping and ice creams out of small children's hands.'

When Blunkett became an MP in 1987, Ruby's successor, Ted, a Labrador cross, became the first guide dog to assist a Member of Parliament. Blunkett speaks to *Political Animals* in a meeting room in the House of Lords with his current guide dog sat quietly at his feet. Barley, a retriever/German shepherd cross, is a remarkable and incredibly intelligent political animal and the sixth guide dog to assist Blunkett in his parliamentary roles. 'Barley is the best all-rounder I've had,' says Blunkett.

> Each guide dog I've had has had their own characteristics and their own special ways of doing things, and some are excellent at one thing and some another. This dog has been pretty well excellent at everything. And given the waiting lists for new dogs – my dog, as we're recording this interview, is coming up to nine years old – I want him to work, if he can, if he's fit enough, and if he's still willing, for another couple of years.

I met Blunkett just a few days after he had been to see Prime Minister Sir Keir Starmer in Downing Street. 'I was in No. 10 and Larry the cat was prowling – I imagine that's the term – in the lobby. He hopped onto the windowsill to get out of Barley's way and gave him, in the description of the attendants, "the dark eye" … Barley was completely unfazed by it all.'

Blunkett is a working peer and most weeks spends four days at the House of Lords, where Barley is an invaluable navigator around its ancient corridors. As we descend a narrow spiral staircase, Blunkett points out to me how slowly and deliberately Barley guides him around. 'Over the years, I've learned it's really important not to refuse people's assistance when clearly that would be advantageous to you. I am very open to that now, but the dog allows me to make the choice of when I think I need help, rather than being helpless,' he says.

His dogs have been incredibly important to Blunkett as he connects with the public, a working politician to this day.

The great thing about having a guide dog is that it broke the ice. There were people who would otherwise probably have been quite diffident about speaking to me when I was travelling or on the street, who would find it easier to talk about the dog, and, by talking about the dog, could then start asking about politics, or get into a discussion which otherwise wouldn't have taken place.

Had I sussed out in my teens that having a dog would have been quite attractive in making relationships with the opposite sex, I think I might have had a more fun time.

I've never minded talking about the dog. People say, 'Please excuse me. I know that you have people asking you these questions all the time, and you must get sick of it.' And I actually haven't got sick of it. I quite like the idea that the dog is a conduit for opening up avenues of conversation and allowing people to approach me in a way that they wouldn't otherwise be able to do.

However, not all of his dogs have been without controversy. When Blunkett was leader of Sheffield Council in the 1980s, his second guide dog, the aforementioned Ted, caused something of a royal stir.

> The Queen had come to open new facilities. We served her the most undrinkable tea I've ever had. I took a sip of it and realised I should have tested it beforehand. I was holding a cup of this undrinkable tea, the Queen was carrying hers as she was coming round, shaking hands, and Ted was nuzzling up to the Queen and virtually knocked the tea out of her grasp.
>
> She was very understanding about it. I did say to her afterwards that it was probably a good thing. If he hadn't [knocked her], she would have been in the embarrassing situation of taking a sip and finding it unacceptable. I don't quite know what we'd done to it, because we pride ourselves in Yorkshire on being able to make decent tea.

Ted was clearly a character, with many of his scrapes detailed in Blunkett's autobiography, *On a Clear Day*. On one occasion, shortly after Blunkett became an MP, Ted had a particularly visceral reaction to a Conservative Budget.

> I think it was when Ted was ageing, and it was the Budget of March 1988 – Nigel Lawson's famous tax-cutting Budget that actually did lead to quite a deep recession. In the middle of the Budget statement, where people are supposed to listen to it entirely without disruption and interruption, my dog was sick.

Dennis Skinner, nicknamed the Beast of Bolsover and well known for his amusing interruptions, in a very loud voice said, 'Who's going to clear up this mess?' And nobody was sure whether he was referring to what Nigel Lawson was proposing or what the dog had just deposited.

A later dog, Lucy, a retriever cross, garnered a rebuke from Speaker Betty Boothroyd for vomiting during a speech by Conservative MP David Willetts attacking Blunkett's policies. Despite this incident, Lucy proved a very useful companion when Blunkett visited schools as Education Secretary.

> Lucy made me a better politician in relating to young people. When I was Education and Employment Secretary, I'd receive a much warmer welcome in schools than I would have otherwise. Some children were afraid of the dog, but most were quite in awe of her and what she was able to do.

Blunkett's dogs were also a welcome distraction for his staff, particularly when things got tough politically during his time in government.

> In the eight years I was in Cabinet, the tension and stress were obviously very great on the staff in the private office and special advisers. Having a dog around was a good thing. Staff were often willing to take the dog for a walk to make sure the dog got out, so it was a relaxation for them too. It was a comfort and an emotional prop for those working around me. So I think the dog did some good.

However, being at the top of government can be gruelling not just for politicians but for dogs too.

> Where I live now we're very close to an ancient woodland and being able to get back and release the dog to run free and to just be a dog and enjoy himself is great for reducing his stress. I am mindful that any guide dog working in London is going to be under much greater pressure than in other parts of the country, just because it's so much busier.
>
> Dogs tell you when they've had enough. Clearly if they become ill, you have absolutely no choice but to retire them. But they do give you an indication when they've slowed down and when they no longer are enjoying the work.

Lucy really did accompany him absolutely everywhere. When Blunkett visited the set of the soap opera *EastEnders*, Lucy even had the honour of meeting actors Patsy Palmer (Bianca) and Sid Owen (Ricky) on the set of the Queen Vic pub. Sadly, Patsy/Bianca did not adapt her trademark phrase 'Rickkkaayy!' to 'Lucaaayy!'

There have sadly, but inevitably, been times when Blunkett has had to say a final goodbye to the companions who have served him so well for many years.

> Cosby, who is the predecessor to my current dog, Barley, got liver cancer when he was seven and we had to handle that and take very careful advice on whether this was going to be operable. I spoke to the vet, who I'd known for many, many years, and he had a similar situation where he tried to save his dog and had found it impossible to do so with exactly the

same circumstances. And he said to me, 'You'll be doing the dog a service if you have him put to sleep.' So I went to the animal hospital – and I make no bones about it – I took one of his balls to put in front of him, I held him while they gave him the injection and then I cried.

And it's just one of those occasions where I was just remembering with affection a dog that was a character. I mean, there were some mornings where he would, in his own way, say, 'I don't really want to do it today.' And I would have to say to him, 'I'm afraid you've got no choice. Yes, we're off, and I'm going to make sure you do the job.' He was a very lovable, massive dog at forty-six kilos. Goodness, and a real character, and I miss him enormously.

Blunkett reflects movingly in his autobiography on the death of Ted some years earlier. Teddy, as he was also known, fell ill in 1988 and died in his master's arms. Blunkett writes of never having been a real sentimentalist before, but Teddy changed that. He also included the following poem, which he penned in memory of Teddy:

> He was a gentle giant of a dog,
> Running magnificent through the woods,
> A huge branch clamped between his teeth
> He was a soft, lovable lion of a dog,
> Full of sniffs and a nuzzling nose,
> Touching against the hand
> To say thank you for walks
> And for fondling of ears.

He was a *Guinness Book of Records* dog,
First ever in the Chamber,
Enduring the noise and bad behaviour
Of the 'schoolboys',
And the medieval ritual of the Mother of Parliaments.
He was a TV star dog,
Sleeping through *Question Time*,
Lifting his head only when it was time to go,
And bringing a smile to millions
And joy to those who knew him well.

A child could climb upon his back
Or pull his ears without fear or threat,
For Teddy was a dog of love, you see,
Who cared for others as he cared for me.
Guiding me, wherever I needed to be,
Full of keenness, enthusiasm and love of life,
Working to a record age
And giving of his best, wherever we might be.
Being superb – my guide dog gave his all
In those twelve years, you see.

And all of us who knew him
Will remember him with gratitude,
And with love and much affection.

Prime Minister Thatcher had sometimes patted Teddy on the head, even though she and Blunkett never debated. She sent Blunkett a condolence card when Teddy died, saying she understood how hard it was to lose a guide dog and how affectionate they are to their owners. Blunkett also received sacks of condolence letters from the public, who donated generously in Teddy's memory to Guide Dogs for the Blind, raising £7,600. The money was used to train new guide dogs, one of which was named Teddy in his honour.

Through Teddy, Blunkett paved the way for a parliamentarian to have a working guide dog assisting them around the Houses of Parliament. In 2013, Chris Holmes, the first (and so far only) British swimmer to win six gold medals at a single Paralympic Games, took up his peerage. He sits on the Conservative benches and his guide dog, Nandy, assists him. In 2024, Steve Darling became a Liberal Democrat MP, and now brings his guide dog Jennie with him to the House of Commons.

'Steve is a very able and long-standing guide dog owner, and has learned his politics like I did – in local government,' says Blunkett.

> I didn't think he needed too many tips, but it was nice to know things were working better for him now than they had when I first came in, back in 1987. There was great suspicion at that time about what the dog might get up to and the disruption [they might cause]. I did point out that the noises that came from the members of the House of Commons, particularly during Prime Minister's Questions, were far greater than any disruption the dog was likely to cause.
>
> Steve Darling got the most enormous social media hit and coverage on his dog Jennie coming into the Palace of Westminster, and I couldn't help but quip that Barley was

extremely jealous. Barley was very kind to Jennie. He gave her a very gentle sniff rather than a growl. But I suspect next time they bump into each other, he might have something to say!

I spoke to Steve Darling on Jennie's sixth birthday, 22 April 2025. A day later, during Prime Minister's Questions, Prime Minister Sir Keir Starmer wished her a happy birthday from the dispatch box. 'I've had Jennie for three years,' says Darling.

> Guide dogs are incredibly highly trained; they can do so many things. They do go through lots of tests and not all of them make it. I was speaking to someone recently who told me, 'Oh, I've got a failed guide dog.' And I was saying to her, 'No, no, it's a fallen angel.'
>
> My world is a bit like looking through frosted glass with a kaleidoscope. It just depends on the conditions. Jennie enjoys wandering around and she always tries to steer me towards two places. One is the Terrace Café, because she is more likely to find food on the floor there than anywhere else. And then the other one is the chamber, because she thinks it is a good place to go and have a good sleep.

Jennie is three-quarters golden retriever and one-quarter Labrador.

> In the first few weeks, the police officers around the Palace [of Westminster] were apparently looking at Jennie as if she was their newborn child. It was really, really positive.
>
> My wife has had four guide dogs, but I've never known a

guide dog to be as sociable as Jennie is. She really loves affection from other people.

Jennie also proved a hit when Darling was campaigning in his Torbay constituency in the July 2024 general election, although her attention has been known to wander. 'Jennie tends to be very fixated on cats, which can be a bit of a distraction. But you soon get her back on track,' says Darling.

The reaction to Jennie has been almost universally positive – with one notable, worrying exception.

> She was bitten by an XL Bully when we were out. It had escaped from somebody's house and was running around the neighbourhood, and it just went straight for her throat. It took four of us to get the dog off of her, even though it wasn't fully grown; it was about the size of a Staffordshire bull terrier.
>
> Jennie had blood dripping down her front. It looked more like a shark bite than anything, but she was still putting a paw up to little kids within twenty minutes as we were waiting for a lift to the vets to be sorted out. She's just such a good-natured dog.

Darling emphasises that no guide dog should be approached or petted when they are working. But when Jennie is out of her harness, she loves being fussed over by Darling's fellow MPs. 'Labour colleagues tell me that they feel that when Jennie goes into the chamber, the temperature does drop – she's a calming influence,' he says.

But the temperature in Westminster dropped to sub-zero on one occasion when Jennie accompanied Darling to Downing

Street. 'Larry was in the window and Jennie was just fixated looking at him, but Larry just sat in the window with his eyes closed, as if to say, "I'm here, but I don't see you, dog."'

Ever the politician, Jennie 'will work the front bench of the Lib Dems', says Darling. But it's not just the Liberal Democrats in Parliament that Jennie is friends with.

> On one infamous occasion, she did spot Jo Baxter, a Labour MP, who knows her quite well because we're both on the Work and Pensions Select Committee. Jennie quickly crossed the chamber to say 'hello', much to the delight of Jo and a couple of other Labour ladies who were on the other side of the chamber.

Baxter is well-known to be an animal lover and is chairwoman of the All-Party Parliamentary Group on Cats. The incident earned Jennie a playful rebuke from Wendy Chamberlain MP, the Liberal Democrat Chief Whip. A tweet included a funny photo of Chamberlain wagging her finger at an oblivious Jennie who had 'crossed the floor', the phrase used to describe when an MP defects to another party. Darling recounts that

> just afterwards, an emergency motion was put forward at our party spring conference berating Wendy for telling Jennie off because, as Liberal Democrats, we believe in cross-party working, and Jennie is a good girl and should be given a treat for trying to foster this approach in the House of Commons. Strangely enough, the motion wasn't selected for debate! But it was good fun.

Many other parliamentarians love Jennie, with the Speaker, Sir Lindsay Hoyle, being a big animal fan himself. 'Jennie recognises the Speaker as somebody who likes engaging with her. He gave her a good fuss after my swearing in as an MP for the first time,' says Darling.

Hoyle himself has a significant menagerie of animals in the Speaker's apartments, all of which are named after iconic British parliamentarians. Maggie the tortoise was unsurprisingly named after former Prime Minister Margaret Thatcher. In 2019, Hoyle, who declined to be interviewed for *Political Animals*, told the BBC, 'She's got a hard shell and she's not for turning. She's three stone in weight is this tortoise.' In May 2020, he tweeted, 'It is no secret that I'm an animal lover – and animals play a vital role in keeping us safe in Parliament.' Hoyle's parrot, Boris – named after Boris Johnson, of course – has the 'propensity to chatter loudly'. Betty, his Patterdale terrier, is named after former Speaker of the House of Commons Betty Boothroyd. Hoyle is also the proud owner of a brown Maine Coon tabby named Attlee, after the post-war Labour leader Clement. On social media, Hoyle described Attlee as 'the boldest, craziest life-force you can imagine. He races around my office, much to the amusement of my team, and brings a smile to the face of doorkeepers, police officers, cleaners – and everyone who comes into contact with him.'

Hoyle's previous cat, Patrick, died in 2022, two years after he was crowned Westminster's top cat in Battersea's 'Purr Minister' competition, having received nearly 5,000 votes. Patrick's manifur-sto pledged 'a better work/mouse balance, empawment for staff, purrfection for all, regular repawts, no fur flying in the chamber, impurrtiality and feline fine moments for everyone'.

As well as the All-Party Parliamentary Group on Cats chaired by Jo Baxter (her deputy is the aptly named Labour MP Cat Eccles) there is also APDAWG, the All-Party Parliamentary Dog Advisory Welfare Group. It was established in 2017 to 'explore, highlight, discuss and challenge dog-related activities, legislation and trends, with the overall aim of improving health and welfare of UK's dogs and dog owners, plus society in general'.

Parliamentarians with dogs are keen participants in the annual Westminster Dog of the Year competition, which has taken place since 1992. Dogs perform exercises and tasks on one of the greens outside Parliament and a combination of the public vote and the judges' vote informs which of them receives the crown. It's not just a lot of fun – it is also an opportunity for the Kennel Club and Dogs Trust to draw the attention of MPs and peers to canine concerns, such as the effect of fireworks on dogs, the importance of dog training and protecting dog walkers. In 2023, Dogs Trust chief executive Owen Sharp told *Politico*, 'It's a fun-filled day out with an important message at its core – helping to promote dog welfare issues and encourage responsible ownership.'

With the exception of the three guide dogs working in Parliament, MPs are discouraged from taking their pets to work, although, in 2016, the persistent rodent problem did inspire the then Minister for Disabled People, Penny Mordaunt, to bring in her cat, Titania, to help. One of her four cats at the time – the others were Achilles, Polaris and Betelgeuse – Titania's trip to Westminster was characterised by Mordaunt's spokesman as 'not a permanent fixture, but [the cat] made a mouse-deterring visit and proved very popular'. Mordaunt herself tweeted that as 'a great believer in credible deterrence, I'm applying the principle to the lower ministerial corridor mouse problem'. Sadly, the Commons authorities were not so amused, with the Serjeant-at-Arms warning Mordaunt not to bring the cat for a return visit.

A House of Commons spokeswoman said, 'The only animals allowed in Parliament are guide dogs or security dogs; anyone who brings in an animal that doesn't meet these criteria is reminded of the policy and gently asked not to do it again.'

And in June 2025, Palace of Westminster authorities rejected a Labour peer's call to bring in cats to control the vermin problem. The senior deputy speaker, Lord Gardiner of Kimble, replied to Lord Berkeley's written question by pointing out there was too much construction on the decaying estate to provide a safe living environment for a free-roaming cat, that cats could be trapped by self-closing doors and that there were no arrangements for daily cat care that could reasonably be made.

All of which is a bit of a shame, really.

PART VI

REFLECTING ON POLITICAL ANIMALS

CHAPTER SEVENTEEN

THE POLLSTER AND THE PSYCHOTHERAPIST

In my job as a presenter on the Talk radio and TV network, I speak to people across the country numerous times a week. While the people who lift the phone to ring, tweet, text or send a voice note are not scientifically representative of the country at large, I believe they are representative of those who listen to and watch Talk, and I love hearing from them whatever their opinion. On my shows, as has become my catchphrase, we try to disagree without being disagreeable.

The powerhouse behind my former on-air feature 'Cat of the Week' was my technical operator and trusty sidekick Dave Rhodes. Better known as 'Tech Op Dave', he is the man tasked with keeping everything running smoothly by pressing all the right buttons (whereas, as an arts graduate, I am kept well away from any buttons). Lots of people have shared their animal stories with us over the years, both serious and not so serious. However, I'm still left wondering how people really feel about animals, particularly political animals.

Like Talk, social media is a window into public opinion, but it is not particularly scientific. As David Cameron once said, 'Twitter is not Britain.' He also said, which he perhaps instantly regretted, that 'too many tweets makes a tw**'. Sometimes a major event or social media pile-on can feel huge when in reality it is not. Many online observers were convinced, for example, that Donald Trump couldn't possibly win the 2016 or 2024 presidential elections or that the Brexit vote would never go through, because their social media feeds, helped by platforms' algorithms, reinforced their world view. (Cats and dogs aren't usually up for election – although tell that to the people of Talkeetna, Alaska, who elected Stubbs the cat their honorary mayor from July 1997 until his death in 2017.)

Once described by *The Times* as 'the lantern-jawed, housewives' favourite pollster', Joe Twyman is the co-founder of Deltapoll, one of the UK's largest polling companies. Usually, Twyman's firm charges businesses, governments and media organisations tens of thousands of pounds to conduct a poll. Luckily, as my budget for *Political Animals* was slightly smaller than that of, say, the UK government, he did it for a steak dinner. 'But please make it clear it has to be a large steak,' Twyman insists.

For this book, Twyman and his Deltapoll colleagues interviewed 1,524 British adults online between 4 and 7 April 2025. The data has been weighted to be representative of the British adult population as a whole.

First up, and perhaps unsurprisingly, the survey revealed that the most famous political animal in the UK today is Larry the cat. Overall, 47 per cent of respondents had heard of him, which can be broken down to 45 per cent of men and 49 per cent of women. For Gen Z, it's 27 per cent, rising to 39 per cent for millennials and 47 per cent for Gen X. It's Baby Boomers who know him best, however, 64 per cent of them recognising Larry. Around 60 per cent of Conservative, Reform UK and Liberal Democrat voters know him, falling to 47 per cent amongst Labour voters.

The other cats of Westminster are less well known by some margin. The Treasury's cat, Gladstone, is known by only about 11 per cent of voters, whereas Palmerston the Foreign Office cat (now in Bermuda) is known by 7 per cent of the population. Steve Darling's guide dog Jennie and Boris Johnson's dog Dilyn are known by just 6 per cent of the population.

The UK is a nation of pet lovers, though, with 55 per cent of those polled telling Twyman and his team they have an animal: 32 per cent have a dog, 28 per cent have a cat and 6 per cent have a fish. Worryingly, 2 per cent of people said they didn't know if they had a pet – they should probably find out!

When asked whether they would have a more or less favourable attitude towards a politician who owned a pet, 16 per cent said they would think of the politician more favourably, but a whopping 74 per cent said it would make no difference, rising to 88 per cent in the over-65 category. The results were almost exactly the same when Deltapoll asked respondents for their views on a politician having a husband or wife and again when it came to them having children: 18 per cent felt more favourably, but, again, most people, 72 per cent, said it makes no difference.

However, if we break this down into the public's view on particular species, the results are a bit different. When asked how they would feel about a politician if they owned a dog, 60 per cent said they would think more favourably, with 28 per cent saying it would make no difference, while 12 per cent said they would feel less favourably. As for a cat-owning politician, 52 per cent of those polled said they would think of them more favourably and 13 per cent less favourably, while 33 per cent said it wouldn't affect their opinion one way or the other.

Sir Gavin Williamson, dad to Cronus the tarantula, will be fascinated to see that 52 per cent of people say it makes no difference to their view of a politician if they have a spider, with 20 per cent saying they would think of the politician more favourably and 26 per cent less favourably. Sadly for Cronus, she only has 1 per cent name recognition amongst the public, but then she has been out of public life for a little while. Meanwhile, 24 per cent of people said they would think less favourably of a politician if they had a snake.

As someone who campaigns for animals to be rescued rather than bought (I frequently tweet the hashtag #AdoptDontShop), I was particularly interested in the public's attitude to politicians who adopt rescue animals, such as Boris Johnson's Dilyn. When asked by Deltapoll, 'Generally speaking, do you think you would have a more favourable attitude to a politician who had a rescue pet from an animal shelter, a pet bought from a breeder or does it make no difference?', more than half (61 per cent) said they would think more favourably if the pet came from an animal shelter, with just 13 per cent saying they would favour a politician who had a bought pet. A further 23 per cent said it would make no difference and 3 per cent said they didn't know.

The results from some key electoral demographics are worthy of note here. Of the women polled, 67 per cent said they would view a rescue pet-owning politician more favourably, against 9 per cent for one with a pet from a breeder. In the over-65 category – the part of the electorate most likely to go out and vote on polling day – 91 per cent of respondents felt more favourably about a rescue pet owner, but none had a higher opinion of the owner of a pet from a breeder. Of the hard-to-reach 18–24-year-old group,

64 per cent said they liked politicians more if they had a rescue animal.

'Larry the cat scores quite highly,' says Twyman, reflecting on the survey results.

> Overall, dogs are favoured over cats – but only just and it's within the margin of error.
>
> A strong majority of nearly three-quarters say that a politician having a pet makes no difference to them, broadly in line with the other things we tested – except having a professional career before entering politics. Even then, more than half say that doesn't make a difference.
>
> Of those for whom it does make a difference, dogs come top of the favourability charts – again, just ahead of cats. The people are less enthusiastic about rabbits and horses, divided over spiders and slightly against snakes.
>
> If politicians are going to make the most from having an animal, the key seems to be to have adopted it from a rescue shelter and then to let young people and over-65s know you have it. That is where approval numbers are at their highest.

It certainly is striking that people notice whether a politician has an animal, but it doesn't influence their behaviour as much as other factors. Psychotherapist and broadcaster Lucy Beresford agrees with Sir Tony Blair, who wrote in his autobiography, *A Journey*: 'The hardest thing for a politician to understand is most people, most of the time, don't give politics a thought all day long.'

'If we were in the middle of a campaign and we were seeing

politicians out with their dog, stroking cats, stroking horses, I do wonder whether the findings might have been slightly different,' Beresford tells *Political Animals*. I ask her about our relationship with animals as a whole and how our pets can help us express ourselves as a nation, not least politically. 'There is definitely a whole generation of people who only cried at *Lassie* films, but they didn't cry at any other time. They didn't feel that they had permission to do that, apart from in the confines of a cinema watching a movie about a heroic dog.'

Beresford points out the British have historically been reluctant to show their vulnerability, but that this can be acceptably manifested towards animals. 'Showing vulnerability towards your horse, towards your golden retriever, towards your black Labrador, was, in a way, an acceptable form of showing affection, showing that you could be kind and nurturing and loving,' says Beresford.

> And I think that's what happens even nowadays. People instinctively feel that if you have a pet, particularly a traditional pet, by which I mean a dog or a cat, people assume you must also be a very kind person, a very nurturing person, a very thoughtful person, very compassionate. Obviously, we know people who own animals that aren't like that, but there's a general perception that, 'Oh, you've got an animal in your life. You must be OK. You must be a decent human being.' But a dog is for life, not just for political campaigns.

Beresford also says animals can be helpful when it comes to working out what we make of new people.

From an anthropological point of view, on a pre-verbal level, we want to make a judgement about someone and whether they're safe and reliable and trustworthy before we even start to speak to them. You need to remember that politicians in particular have got a very strong reason, probably more than most, to make you like them as quickly as possible. So they might kind of co-opt animals to strengthen those positive associations.

I don't think it was any great surprise in that particular finding that actually the majority of people think that getting a rescue pet from a shelter is probably going to make you think more favourably about the politician. Partly, that is because that makes you seem a bit more relatable, because it's not an expensive way of getting your pet, and therefore it's something that people think, 'Oh, well, that makes me think that you're a bit like me, that you're not going to a really expensive breeder, you're not going for a really expensive type of breed of dog or cat, and therefore, you're more normal even if I have never met you.'

It's as if the politician is saying: 'I'm a normal person and I want to have an animal in my house, and I'm now going to do this noble thing – this sort of slightly more compassionate thing – which is to rescue a pet that's been abandoned or mistreated.' So there's a different story that's being told. Because everything is about the stories that we tell each other and the stories we tell ourselves about other people.

As referenced in Chapter Five, in September 2020, as Joe Biden challenged Donald Trump for the highest office in the USA, a group calling itself Dog Lovers For Joe put out an ad highlighting that Trump had been the first President for over a century not to have a dog in the White House. The ad urged dogs to 'choose your human wisely'. Beresford reflects that

> it was an incredibly authentic response from Donald Trump to say, 'I've never had a dog. I don't see why I should get a dog now, just for political purposes.' And I think in this day and age when the electorate is arguably a little bit more psychologically savvy and has a lot more information to work on when casting a vote, the idea that someone isn't going to play the game does appeal to a lot of voters.

Beresford points out that Obama didn't have a dog when he was elected to the White House, yet felt he needed to get one – even if that was more about fulfilling a promise to his daughters.

> Obama ended up getting a very particular type of dog that was very hypoallergenic, but of course, almost by definition, they couldn't get it from a rescue shelter. And he did get quite a bit of flack for not having a rescue dog. But in that moment, you can see, first of all, how it can go very badly wrong and how you can get negative publicity.
>
> But secondly, it kind of reinforces Donald Trump's view, which is 'Why should I get a dog when I've never had a dog?' This is just ridiculous posturing. And I think a lot of people felt that actually, that was more authentic to take that stance.

Beresford has also analysed Twyman's polling data for *Political Animals* from a psychological perspective.

> What I was struck by in the results from Deltapoll was that, on the whole, people felt it was only of marginal significance to have a pet. What was far more important for people was whether somebody had had a professional career before politics. I think voters are making more judicious judgements about their politicians. And I think there's a primitive sense of 'I want my leader to have a pet', but as the Trump scenario demonstrates, actually, is it going to stop you getting into power – and is it going to stop you getting into power twice? No.

Of course, not all politicians share stories of their relationship with animals to highlight their compassionate and caring side. South Dakota governor Kristi Noem was one of the leading contenders to be Trump's running mate until she wrote in her memoir about killing one of her dogs. In *No Going Back: The Truth on What's Wrong with Politics and How We Move America Forward*, Noem noted that Cricket the dog 'had come to us from a home that struggled with her aggressive personality'. On a day's hunting at Noem's ranch, Cricket did not do what she was told, scaring birds out of the range of those who wanted to shoot them and disobeying orders. On their way back, Cricket killed some chickens at a neighbour's farm, and tried to bite Noem when she attempted to catch her. Noem wrote in her memoir:

> I hated that dog. At that moment, I realised I had to put her down ... This was my dog and my responsibility, and I would not ask someone else to clean up my mess. I stopped the truck in the middle of the yard, got my gun, grabbed Cricket's leash

and led her out into the pasture and down into the gravel pit … It was not a pleasant job, but it had to be done.

She also decided to kill the family goat, much to the surprise of some farm workers, claiming the goat was 'nasty and mean … It's often messy, ugly, and matter-of-fact, dealing with a problem that no one wants to deal with.'

'Noem openly talks about shooting the dog dead, which is something that she herself did, and that killed her campaign completely overnight,' says Beresford.

She couldn't understand that. They lived on the land. They were farming people, which, of course, is also part of the British psyche. But she was not a contender the following day.

I think it's about almost gloating about the fact that you'd killed your own dog. There is a certain type of person, even nowadays, where dogs are actually not pets. They are working animals. They live outside the house. They live in cages. The first time I saw some friends of mine and saw that they kept their two dogs in a cage outside, I found that really uncomfortable.

Despite this story, Noem was appointed by Trump to be his Homeland Security Secretary, a non-elected role. So even this revelation, which many find harsh and even repugnant, was no bar to high office. In June 2025, the Reform UK turned independent MP Rupert Lowe revealed he had had his seventeen-year-old Labrador, Cromwell, shot rather than having him put down by a vet. Cromwell had lost the use of his back legs, and Lowe, a landowner, asked his gamekeeper to shoot the dog. In response to the backlash, Lowe argued it was more humane as it saved Cromwell what Lowe believed would be a traumatic visit to a vet. He also said it was common practice in rural communities.

Noem was not the only White House wannabe who had a questionable record when it came to animals. Robert F. Kennedy Jr, an independent candidate, became US Health Secretary under President Trump in 2025. In August 2024, Kennedy posted a three-minute Twitter video outlining how he had dumped a bear cub carcass in Central Park in New York City in 2014. He detailed how he was in upstate New York when a driver in front of him hit and killed the cub. Kennedy intended to skin the bear and eat the meat. Running late for a flight, he decided to leave the animal in Central Park along with a bicycle that a friend had asked him to get rid of. The body of the six-month-old cub, which weighed 44 pounds, was found by a dog walker, but it was only a decade later, when running for President, that Kennedy cleared up the mystery, confessing it was him who had dumped the bear.

In 2016, former UK Deputy Prime Minister Michael Heseltine clarified a story from the 1990s that he had strangled his mother's Alsatian to death. Originally, Lord Heseltine told *Tatler*, 'I went to stroke him and he started biting me. If you have a dog that turns, you just cannot risk it. So I took Kim's collar – a sort of choker chain – and pulled it tight. Suddenly he went limp.' This was interpreted at the time, and for many years afterwards, as Heseltine having killed the animal. In 2016, he clarified the story, telling the Press Association, 'I didn't strangle the dog. They have misunderstood. The dog was perfectly all right after this incident.' However, the dog was put down the next day, having experienced what Heseltine believes to have been 'a kind of mental breakdown' before the original incident. He says he was told that he 'had no choice' as the animal was dangerous.

Ten years earlier, in 2006 in the Russian city of Sochi, Vladimir Putin used the presence of a dog to intimidate a political opponent, Angela Merkel. The Russian President and German Chancellor were giving a press conference together and Putin brought along his large black Labrador, Koni. It was well known that Merkel is scared of dogs, having been attacked by one in 1995. Putin later denied that he knew this, but she wrote in her 2024 memoir *Freedom* that she believed Russian officials were well aware of her canine fear. Merkel added that she did not accept Putin's apology at the time, claiming the presence of the dog was a clear 'power play' to 'test' her.

'It's a story that she herself tells that obviously felt so unbelievably psychologically manipulative that someone would put another person in a situation that remobilises their fears, their very worst fears of a threat of being harmed or being, perhaps, even extinguished,' says Beresford.

> And that's a really brutal power play and Putin, I fear, is just very, very good at those.
>
> Putin uses animals to tap into a very primitive narrative. So when he is seen bare-chested on a horse it is very much about presenting himself as this archetypal strong man from an earlier age, a pre-car age. 'I'm harking back to the great days of Russia and Catherine the Great times. I'm bare-chested to emphasise my virility.' To some extent, horses can also do that because they

have such huge penises. In mythology, horses are about potency and strength and stamina. So Putin is definitely trying to harness that when he has these photo opportunities in the woods.

As discussed in Chapter Two, many world leaders use animals as presents for their contemporaries, but China in particular is known for its panda diplomacy. The Chinese Communist Party's first gift of pandas was to the Soviet Union to mark the fortieth anniversary of the October Revolution in 1957. Between 1958 and 1982, China presented twenty-three pandas to nine different countries. Most famously, Mao gave Richard Nixon two pandas in Beijing in 1972, on the first visit by a US President to the People's Republic. Ling-Ling and Hsing-Hsing went to live in the National Zoo in Washington DC, attracting 20,000 visitors on their first day alone. Less well-known is Nixon's reciprocal gift to the Chinese: a pair of Musk oxen. Two years later, the UK Prime Minister Sir Edward Heath made it clear when he visited China that he, too, would like a pair of pandas. Chia-Chia and Ching-Ching arrived at London Zoo soon afterwards and also proved to be a huge hit with visitors. More recently, Brigitte Macron, the wife of the French President, became 'godmother' to a panda lent by the Chinese to Paris Zoo, and in 2024 the US National Zoo in Washington DC welcomed two new pandas, Bao Li and Qing Bao, their first in twenty-four years.

Other examples of diplomacy involving animals include the pure-bred Akhal-Teke stallion given to British Prime Minister John Major by President Saparmurat Niyazov of Turkmenistan in 1993. It took six months of negotiations to establish how Maksat would be transported to the UK. He was put on a train to Moscow, where there was a complicated attempt at bribing customs officials with a truckload of large yellow melons. The animal kicked and bit his handlers and was very ill-tempered through the journey, not least because of the toothache from which he was suffering. Bandits also attacked the convoy as they passed through Kazakhstan. Maksat was meant to join the household cavalry but was deemed unsuitable and the UK army eventually gave the horse to Lorna Winn-Jones in Carmarthenshire in Wales.

'Maksat came to me in 1996 a sad, confused and troubled little horse with a few health issues, but he blossomed into a powerful and confident stallion who seems happy in his adopted home of Wales,' she recalled in an interview with WalesOnline in 2012. Maksat later won awards and qualified for the British Dressage Championships.

In 2013, French President François Hollande was presented with a camel for helping drive Islamist extremists from Mali. Left in the care of a local family, the camel was intended to be vaccinated and sent to a French zoo, but the family 'looking after' the animal slaughtered it and ate the meat.

In a more successful case of animal diplomacy, French President Emmanuel Macron gave Xi Jinping an eight-year-old gelding called Vesuvius from France's elite Republican Guard in January 2018. The Chinese President had inspected the French cavalry during a 2014 visit and was given the horse as a symbol of French excellence and respect.

'Giving the gift of an animal, particularly between one government and the other, might seem like a really beautiful way to cement a relationship, particularly if the animal in question ... is a very respected creature in that culture,' says Beresford.

The problem is that it takes a lot of upkeep to look after one of these very special creatures, and what happens if it dies? Does that mean that the relationship has now ended? And in particular, what happens if you mistreat the animal, or if you don't look after it to the high levels that your donor has expected? Therein lies the very fraught layers of diplomacy you have with many gifts.

Gifts are not just about what is actually given. They tell you much more about the giver, and if somebody is giving you that very special gift but it's going to require an awful lot of work, the giver is saying, 'I expect you to really, really work hard for this friendship.'

On a lighter note, I asked Beresford for her evaluation of Larry, the best-known political animal in the UK according to Deltapoll. What did Beresford make of Larry's fame?

> I think there's a 'keep calm and carry on', no-fuss dimension to Larry and his longevity. Of course, that kind of Dunkirk spirit of 'I'm going to see off all of these different Prime Ministers'. You know, 'I've got the longevity that they never had'. Larry doesn't really care who he's meeting.
>
> I think he also has benefited from being the cat that … came of age in the social media era. So he's been able to communicate with his audience in a way that previous pets were not able to do. They've always had to have that mediated by their owners, whereas Larry is able to speak directly to his fans.

AFTERWORD

Both the United States and the United Kingdom are nations of animal lovers. It's clear their political animals have always been popular too. What I didn't quite appreciate when embarking on this book was just how loved and cherished Larry and other political animals are by people who may never meet them. Politicians such as Richard Nixon may have sometimes cynically used animals to soften their image, and that may even happen today. But at least politicians are attempting to connect with a public that may not love them but that certainly love animals.

I've also been inspired by politicians (yes, really) who have very busy lives running the country yet still make time to ensure they rescue animals. Others fight for animal welfare, such as Green Party member of the Scottish Parliament Mark Ruskell, who rescued Bert the greyhound and then embarked on a campaign to ban greyhound racing in Scotland. 'Bert is a very gentle soul and has fitted in very well with the family,' Ruskell told Scotland's *Sunday Mail* in April 2025. Ruskell also detailed how Bert has to have the light kept on when he sleeps at night – probably due to having been born in a puppy farm where lights are almost always kept on – as well as the trauma and injury Bert received from his time as a racing greyhound. Clearly, Ruskell is giving Bert a wonderful retirement from the challenges the greyhound faced while his dad campaigns for other dogs not to be put through the same thing.

As a long-time advocate for adopting animals rather than shopping from breeders, it is wonderful to see the boost rescue homes such as Battersea Dogs & Cats Home have received from some of the political animals featured in this book. Indeed, Battersea has erected a blue plaque beside Larry's former pen in recognition of all that he's done for them. Other political animals have inspired other people to adopt or donate money to their former rescue centres.

Battersea identifies 'working cats', which are less suited to a domestic home setting. Also called 'outlet cats', they are rehomed to an environment that best suits them, where they can live more independently and they can come and go as they please, such as on a farm or at a stables or garden centre. There is less pressure on these cats to interact directly with people. The centre says that typically a Battersea working cat will require less maintenance than a domestic pet and requires someone to simply ensure they have food, water and appropriate shelter. This certainly fits the model of a number of Westminster cats, although it seemed to work less well for Gladstone and better for Larry.

While there is little chance of President Trump bringing an animal into the White House during his final term there, on this side of the Atlantic there is the tantalising prospect of more political animals in Whitehall. Despite the fact that the Secretary of State for Scotland Ian Murray has been very unkind about Larry, calling him 'the most miserable animal you'll ever meet in your life' and 'a little s***', the prospect has been raised of the Scotland Office getting its own cat. Just up Whitehall from Downing

Street, the Scotland Office would be a great home for a rescue cat, though little has been heard about the idea since it was first reported by *The Spectator* in December 2024.

I have focused on the political animals of Washington and Westminster in this book. But I've also received sad news during the writing process from another part of the Commonwealth: Canada. Coal, the final resident of the cat sanctuary at Parliament Hill in Ottawa, Canada, died in July 2025. Volunteers fed and looked after the feral cats like Coal and his friends from the 1970s to 2013. The Parliament Hill cats are descended from those who were used as rodent catchers in the Parliament buildings as far back as the 1920s. By the 1950s, with advances in chemical pest control, the cats were shooed outside. Eventually, a colony was established by a few generous people and the Ottawa Humane Society. A man called René Chartrand built little houses for the cats to sleep in. The cats were all spayed or neutered by 1998, and by 2013, only Coal and three others remained. They were then adopted by volunteers, with Danny Taurozzi taking Coal. Something of a celebrity cat in Canada, with a huge social media following, Coal often visited elderly people in care homes. Jacob Hall, a former Parliament Hill colony contributor, now runs a fan account for Prime Minister Mark Carney's cat, Nico. 'I made the account to add some positivity, lighten the mood of the political climate and have a little fun,' Jacob tells *Political Animals*. He is also assembling a world cat Cabinet involving Larry, Palmerston, Willow Biden and others.

Like Jacob, I got to know some less famous political animals in my career. Until 2022, the Belfast headquarters of the Northern Ireland Office (NIO) was at Stormont House. Between 2016 and

2018, I worked there as special adviser to the Secretary of State for Northern Ireland, James Brokenshire. It was a tough job, but I had a smile on my face every morning when I went in and saw Furbie, Maggie and Ginger, feral cats who were fed every morning by the security guards at around the same time that I tended to come through the security gates. I quickly became attached to them. Furbie sadly died at the grand old age of twenty-three in April 2019 and Ginger passed away soon after.

Many political leaders over the years encountered the cats. Martin McGuinness, who was Deputy First Minister of Northern Ireland, used to jokingly call them 'the securocats' – adapting the word 'securocrats', a portmanteau of 'security' and 'bureaucrat' – which he used to level at NIO officials to whom his party objected. Some NIO employees were less concerned with the cats. After explaining how they lived and were looked after at Stormont House to a number of colleagues, I remember my former co-special adviser Lord (Jonathan) Caine remarking, 'I've learned more about those cats in the last two minutes than in the last six years of working here.'

The cats were actually involved in political controversy: they were the unlikely victims of the collapse of the Stormont institutions. A kind retired civil servant in her late seventies, Edna Watters, and her friends Carol and Ron Edmondson came to the Stormont estate for years to look in on and feed the cats alongside the security guards, whatever the weather. But for a time they were denied access for being a 'security risk'. The ridiculous row was soon sorted out and the pensioners, who were no more a security risk than the cats they fed, returned to see their furry friends. The former First Minister Arlene Foster, an animal lover herself, even got involved.

When the NIO moved out of Stormont House in 2022, there was a big question about where Maggie, the surviving cat, would go. She was adopted by a lovely civil servant called Rosemary with whom I used to work. 'We decided to move her to my house to see how she coped,' says Rosemary.

> Having lived all her life outside, I thought I could put her in the garage, but that was never going to happen. So into the dining room she went. My cat Donal was very interested, so we gradually moved them closer until they could eat together. I have to say, he is an absolute gentleman. He still lets her eat first and has what is left. Although he does have his moments, Maggie just glares at him with her famous look, as though she is saying, 'Do you know who I am?'
>
> She is funny and has a lovely personality. I know now why we had so many security staff so keen to feed the cat! Honestly, she is so demanding. She loves spending long summer days in the sun; when it gets dark, in she comes. She enjoys watching television, not least the Eurovision Song Contest and a bit of Talk on the telly too.

It's people like Rosemary, the unsung heroes of this book, who look after many of the political animals, including those who have retired from their duties. Like any animal carer, this is a commitment far greater than simply working alongside an animal in Whitehall or Washington and it is to be lauded. But the political animals I have written about are almost always loved by so many, even those who just work down the corridor.

'I think people forget that actually, civil servants pay out of their own pocket to look after the animals of Whitehall,' says Sonia Khan, a great friend of both Gladstone and Larry.

> I think vets' trips are excluded as most of them come from Battersea, so that is part of the support package, but in terms of day-to-day feeding, toys, snacks and other things.
>
> The cats are meant to be there to weed out all the mice in the offices of Whitehall. But I think, instead, they sort of become pampered celebrities who don't really do anything other than have a wander around and bring joy to the people.

ACKNOWLEDGEMENTS

In July 2016, the *Belfast Telegraph*'s editor Gail Walker commissioned me to write an article about my experiences of the Westminster cats. Reporting for ITV's *Good Morning Britain* in Downing Street, I had posted a few photographs of Palmerston and Gladstone on Twitter. I'd always been a huge animal – and particularly cat – person, but this was the first time I'd written about them for a newspaper. A number of articles for a variety of publications followed in the intervening years, and I am perhaps the only person who has been published in both the *Johannesburg Star* and *Your Cat* magazine.

Having met and worked alongside some of the political animals I've written about, the idea for this book had been rolling around my mind for a few years. I mentioned it to James Stephens of Biteback at the launch of a much more serious book on politics he was publishing. Above the noise of the event, James instantly commissioned *Political Animals*. We subsequently had a lunch alongside James's partner in crime, Olivia Beattie, who brilliantly edited my first book, *The Secret Life of Special Advisers*, to bash out the details. Olivia has been similarly helpful with this book. I am grateful to them, my superb editor Rosie Williamson and their colleagues Suzanne Sangster and Nell Whitaker. Namkwan Cho created another great jacket design – for a second time, thanks to Nam, I hope people *do* judge my books by their covers.

Natasha Proietto has been my best friend for over twenty years and is the assiduous, conscientious and diligent researcher of this book. Her success is despite the equally relentless efforts of her three typing prevention officers Bamboo, Max and, perhaps the most imperious cat to inhibit Planet Earth, Bubble, also known as the Emperor. One of these rescue cats, Bubble, even took to sleeping on top of David Blunkett's biography so Tasha could be dissuaded from reading it. Tasha is a wonderfully caring person and her love for animals and deft scholarship has had an impact on almost every page of this book. Any errors are mine alone.

Speaking of book researchers, thank you to Lucia Henwood – my brilliant researcher on *The Secret Life of Special Advisers* – for her superb cameo in *Political Animals* as indexer.

Friends, contacts and Talk viewers and listeners including Michael Crick, Colin Phillips, Sheridan Westlake, Dr Martin Holmes, Jack Elsom, Claire Pearsall, Nigel Howard, Giles Edwards, Noel Rock, Annika Nestius-Brown, Tom Skinner, Carole Stukley, John Doherty and Carolyn Courtney (and her cat Pluckley, who sadly passed over the rainbow bridge as this book was being written) have helped in various ways, including offering good ideas which I have incorporated.

Others in the shadows of politics and in the press offices of some of the organisations quoted in these pages facilitated interviews. I will not mention them all, apart from, for obvious reasons, Battersea's press officer Cat, who lives in Catford with her cat. I would like to thank everyone named in the book as an interviewee and those who wish to remain anonymous, as well as those who kindly allowed me to use their photographs, which include Lord Cameron, Rishi Sunak, Lord McDonald, Baroness Gray, Horatio Lovering, Emma Southard, Justin Ng and Steve Back. I would also like to thank Lord Blunkett for his permission to use his very moving poem about Teddy, his guide dog, which was originally published in *On a Clear Day*. In particular, Joe Twyman's polling was invaluable – that (large) steak arguably paid for itself.

My father, Ken Cardwell, and great friend Michael Selby looked at my raw copy, improving it immensely, occasionally through the brutality that comes with excellent editing: Michael's pithy 'This is not a sentence' and 'Sort out this word lasagne' were classics of their genre.

Talk management at News UK, namely Dennie Morris, Ricky Freelove (who hates cats), Phil Dave (cat dad to Rufus) and Lauren Webster, gave me the support and freedom to write the book. I am also very grateful to all my colleagues, particularly my long-suffering producers Ryan Thrussell (cat dad to Hermione) and Chris Jacobs, as well as their predecessors Gabriella Incalza (cat mum to Luna) and Beth Keeley.

Tech Op Dave himself, Dave Rhodes, was the technological and administrative brains and brawn behind our 'Cat of the Week' feature, keeping cats in the news and prompting many to get in touch saying I should write a book about animals. I must also mention the members of the 'Talk Cat Parents' WhatsApp group, who kept beautiful photos and videos of their moggies flowing over the months I wrote.

More broadly, I would not be half the journalist, writer and broadcaster I am today without Yvette Shapiro, my mentor for over twenty years, who sparked my passion for rescue animals specifically. Yvette is an inspirational dog mum to Muttley and Amber and a lifelong advocate for animals everywhere.

My own typing prevention officer, my rescue cat Jack, was on hand to remind me to take some breaks from typing to play with and stroke him. He also slept beside me some of the time I wrote, keeping me company. Jack remains the best thing in my life and I am so glad I got to write a book about his furry friends.

Saying that, I doubt he will even bother to read it.

INDEX

Abraham, Marc 196
Achilles (cat) 230
Adams, Gerry xiv
Adams, John 42
Adams, John Quincy 43–4
Adams, Louisa 44
Admiral Dewey (guinea pig) 50
Airedale terriers 53–4
Algonquin (horse) 51–2
alligators 43
All-Party Parliamentary Dog Advisory Welfare Group 230
All-Party Parliamentary Group on Cats 228
Almacy, David 84
Alsatians 245
American Society for the Prevention of Cruelty to Animals 45
American Veterinary Medical Association 101
antelopes 55
Ashdown, Paddy 15
Ashton, Emily 107
Atkins, Eirian Walsh 127, 128–9
Attlee (cat) 229
Attlee, Clement 229

badgers 50
Bailey (dog) 149–50,
Bakr al-Baghdadi, Abu 93
Balfour, Arthur 5
Bambi 64
Bao Li (panda) 247
Barley (dog) 218–19, 222, 225–6

Barney (dog) 83–7
Battersea Dogs & Cats Home 106–107, 108, 110, 114, 118, 120, 134, 136–7, 166–9, 171, 174, 186, 189–90, 229, 252, 254
Baxter (dog) 207–208
Baxter, Jo 228, 230
beagles 69–70
bears 37, 42, 55, 245
Belgian Malinois 93
Beresford, Lucy 239–44, 246–9
Berkeley, Lord Tony 231
Bermuda 119–20
Bert (dog) 251–2
Betelgeuse (cat) 230
Betty (dog) 229
bichon frisé 145–8
Biden, James 98–9
Biden, Jill 97–9, 161
Biden, Joe 53, 68, 95–9, 241–2
Biden, Sara 98–9
Bill (hyena) 50
Bimbo (budgerigar) 217
Bishop Doane (guinea pig) 50
von Bismarck, Otto xiv
Blackberry (dog) 55
Blackie (cat) 55
Blackie (dog) 66
Blackjack (dog) 50–51
Black Jack (horse) 67–8
Blair, Cherie xi, 19–20
Blair, Tony 15, 19, 84, 143, 157, 217, 239
Blencathra, Lord 173
Bluebell (parakeet) 64

Blunkett, David 217–26
Bo (dog) 90–91
Bob (cat) 7–8, 15
Bobby (dog) xiv
bobcats 55
Bono 89
Boothroyd, Betty 221, 229
Boris (parrot) 229
Boston Celtics 85
Bouvier des Flandres 76
Brendon, Piers 24, 26, 29, 34–5, 36–7
Brokenshire, James 158, 254
Brown, Gordon 143–4, 157
Brown, Sarah 143–4
Bruce (dog) 53, 73
Bryant, Traphes 66
Buchanan, James 45–6
Buckland, Robert xiii, 216
Buckland, Sian xiii
Buckley, William F. 77
Buddy (dog) 82–3
budgerigars 34, 217
bulldog 24–5, 38–9, 209
Burton, Dan 81–2
Bush, Barbara (First Lady) 78–9
Bush, Barbara (First Daughter) 85
Bush, George H. W. 78–80
Bush, George W. 78, 83–7, 89, 96
Bush, Jenna 85
Bush, Laura 83–7
Butler, R. A. 36
butterflies 25, 26
Butterfly (dog) 66

C. Fred (dog) 78–9
Cadogan, Alexander 38
Caine, Jonathan 254
Caligula 3
camels 248
Cameron, David 148, 165, 168, 172, 178, 180, 183–4, 191, 235
Cameron, Florence 169
Campbell, Alastair 19
canaries 6, 45, 49
Cannon, Joseph G. 51

Carney, Mark 253
Carrol, Louis 72
Carter, Amy 75–6
Carter, Jimmy 75–6
Caruso (dog) 52
Caruso, Enrico 52
Catherine the Great, Empress of Russia 247
Cats Protection xiii
cavapoos 149
Celia Hammond Animal Trust 125, 127
Chamberlain, Wendy 228
Chambers, C. Fred 78
Champ (dog) 95–8
Chan (cat) 74
Charles III, King of the United Kingdom 161
Charlie (dog) 65, 66
Chartrand, René 253
Chartwell 25, 26–8, 34
Checkers (dog) 71–3
Chequers 162–3, 195
Chia-Chia (panda) 247
Chief mouser of the United Kingdom 8, 145, 170–73
Children's National Medical Center 84, 99
Ching-Ching (panda) 247
Chisholm, Carlyn 173
Chorley, Matt 154
Christmas Carol, A 48–9
Churchill, Winston 8–9, 23–39
Churchill, Clementine 25, 27, 28, 30
Cincinnatus (horse) 47
Civil Rights Act 69
Clark, Alan 20
Cleopatra (horse) 42
Cleveland, Frances 49
Cleveland, Grover 49
Clinton, Bill 17, 80, 81–3, 96
Clinton, Chelsea 81, 82
Clinton, Hillary 81, 82
Clipper (dog) 67
Coal (cat) 253
collies 55–6

INDEX

Colonist II (horse) 23
Colville, John 27, 28
Commander (dog) 99
Conan (dog) 93–4
Coolidge, Calvin 41, 55–6, 64
Coolidge, Grace 55
Corbyn, Jeremy 183, 185, 197
Cosby (dog) 222–3
cows 5, 25, 44, 46, 52
Crewe, Marquess of 6
Cricket (dog) 243–4
crickets 216
crocodiles 37
Cromwell (dog) 244–5
Cromwell, Oliver 5
Cronus (tarantula) xi, 213–16, 238
Cuban Missile Crisis 65–6
Cummings, Dominic xiii–xiv, 193–4
Currie, Betty 83
Curtin, John 35–6
Cymro (dog) 6–7

dachshunds 49, 148
Darling, Alistair 143–4, 166
Darling, Maggie 143–4, 166
Darling, Steve 225–9
Dash (dog) 49
Dauban, Laura 121
Day, Christopher 7, 11
D-Day 37
Decker, Jon 85
deer 64–5
Delaware Humane Association 97
Deltapoll 179–80, 236–9, 242–3
Dick (mockingbird) 42
Dickens, Charles 48–9
Diddley, Bo 90
Digger (kangaroo) 24
Dilyn (dog) 148, 150, 160, 163, 185, 193–201, 237, 238
Disraeli, Benjamin 4
Dodo (dog) 25
Dog Lovers For Joe campaign 96, 241–2
Dog Lovers' Party 15
Dogs Trust 230

Donal (cat) 255
Donelson, William 44
donkeys 55, 206
O'Donoghue, Gary 165, 167, 190
Dowden, Oliver 129–30
Dreamies 108, 114–16, 119, 124, 176–7
Dr Johnson (guinea pig) 50
ducks 113
Duke (cat) 6

eagles 38, 43, 45
EastEnders 222
Ebenezer (donkey) 55
Eccles, Cat 230
Ecclestone, Bernie 21
Edmondson, Carol 254
Edmondson, Ron 254
Eisenhower, Dwight D. 63–4, 71
elephants 46
El Gato (cat) 183–4, 197
Eli Yale (macaw) 50
Elizabeth II, Queen of the United Kingdom xv, 184, 187, 199–200, 220
Ellis, Kristen 76
Emhoff, Doug 98
Emily Spinach (snake) 50
Enoch (goose) 55
Escott, Kata 123
Etti-Cat (cat) 11
Evans, Nigel 20–21
Evie (cat) xi, 113–14, 123–132, 150

Facebook 208
Faithful (dog) 47
Fala (dog) 57–9, 66
Farage, Nigel 207–210
Father O'Grady (guinea pig) 50
Fawlty Towers 143
Feller (dog) 63
Fido (dog) 46
Field, Roswell 50
Fighting Bob Evans (guinea pig) 50
Fillmore, Millard 45
fleas 200
Fleay, David 36

Fleischer, Ari 83
Ford, Gerald 74–5, 81
Ford, Susan 75
Forester (dog) 41
Foster, Arlene 255
foxes 25, 124, 175, 188
foxhunting 25, 41
Fraser, Antonia 5
Frazer, Lucy xii
Freya (cat) 144–7
Friends of Animals Wales 193, 196
Frilly (cat) 7
Furbie (cat) 254

Gale, Roger 21–2
Gallagher, Mary 64
Gardiner, Lord John 231
Gardiner, Julia 44
Garfield, James 48–9
Gascoyne-Cecil, Robert 4
geese 55
General, The (horse) 45
German shepherds 53, 67, 93, 95–9, 218
Ginger (cat) 254
Gladstone (cat) 115, 133–9, 169, 237, 252
Gladstone, William Ewart 4, 37–8, 134
goats 49, 244
golden retrievers 74, 226, 240
goldfish 15, 217
Goldsmith, Zac 197
Gore, Al 80
Gove, Michael 146
Graebner, Walter 32–3
Grant, Jesse 47
Grant, Ulysses S. 47
Gray, Sue 114, 123–32
greyhound racing 94, 251–2
greyhounds 48, 94, 251–2
Grim (dog) 48
Grisham, Henry Oren 82
Grits (dog) 75–6
Groban, Josh 97
guide dogs 217–31
Guide Dogs for the Blind Association 217, 225

guinea pigs 50, 64
Guiney, Lisa 131
Gunn, Sheila 18

Haddon, Celia 112, 114, 119, 136–7, 172, 175, 195
Hager, Andrew 43, 48, 53, 54, 67, 70–72, 76–8, 81–4, 90, 94, 97, 99–100
Haines, Joe 13
Hall, Jacob 253
Halle, Kay 36
Hammond, Celia 125, 127
Hammond, Philip 110–11, 137, 148–9
hamsters 64, 145–6
Hancock, Matt 197–8
Hannigan, Bob 63
Harcourt, William 6
Harding, Florence 55
Harding, Warren 53–5
Hardman, Robert 199–200
Harley (dog) 95
Harris, Kamala 97, 159
Harrison, Benjamin 49
Harrison, William Henry 44
Hayes, Lucy 47–8
Hayes, Rutherford B. 47–8, 77
Hayes, Theo 77–8
Heath, Edward 13, 247
Heidi (dog) 63–4
Heiskell, Samuel Gordon 44
Henry VIII, King of England 3
Her (dog) 68–9
Heseltine, Michael 245–6
Heywood, Jeremy 123–4
Heywood, Suzanne 124
Him (dog) 68–9
hippopotamuses 37, 55
Hitler, Adolf 36
Hollande, François 248
Holmes, Chris 225
Hoover, Herbert 53, 56–7, 67
Hope, Christopher 153
House of Cards 213
Hoyle, Lindsay 229
Hsing-Hsing (panda) 247

INDEX

Humphrey (cat) xi, 15–22, 143
Hunt, Jeremy 151–3, 163, 200
Hunt, Lucia 153
Hussein, King of Jordan 17
hyenas 37, 50

Imperial War Museum 7
Incitatus (horse) 3
India (cat) 86
Ingham, Bernard 13
Innocent VIII, Pope 3
Instagram 95, 134–6, 148, 208
International Cat Day 116, 136, 189
Irish setter 63, 73, 92

Jack (dog) 43
Jack (turkey) 46
jackals 36–7
Jack Russells 148, 193–201
Jackson, Alan 84
Jackson, Andrew 44
Javid, Sajid 137, 138, 148–9
Jefferson, Thomas 42
Jennie (dog) 225–9, 237
Jennifer (dog) 33–4
Jock (cat) 27, 34
Jock (dog) xv
Joe (cat) 6
Johnson, Andrew 46
Johnson, Boris xiii, xiv, 148–9, 160, 163, 185, 193–201, 229
Johnson, 'Lady Bird' 70
Johnson, Luci 68, 70
Johnson, Lynda 70
Johnson, Lyndon B. 67, 68–71
John Ty (canary) 45
Joicey, Nicholas 154
Jojo (cat) x, 155, 187, 203–205
Jones, Eileen 196
Jones, George 17
Jones, Kate 146–7
Josiah (badger) 50
Judicial Watch 98
Jumbo (cat) 8–9
Jungle Book, The 24

kangaroos 24
Kelly, Denis 31
Kelly, Megyn 93
Kelly, Niall 46, 47, 48–9, 54, 55, 78
Kennedy, Caroline 64–5, 66, 67
Kennedy, Jacqueline 64–5, 66–7, 68
Kennedy, John F. 64–8, 91
Kennedy, John Jr 66
Kennedy, Joseph 67
Kennedy, Robert F., Jr 245
Kennedy, Ted 90
Kennel Club 200, 230
Kennerly, David 74
Kermit the Frog 81
Khan, Ayub 66
Khan, Sonia 115, 137–9, 186–7, 256
Khrushchev, Nikita 65
King, Laura 149
Kingman, John 134
King Timahoe (dog) 73
King Tut (dog) 57
Kipling, Rudyard 24
Koni (dog) 84, 246
Kwarteng, Kwasi 150

Labradors 12, 82, 84, 151–3, 157–63, 207–211, 225–9, 240, 244, 246
Laddie Boy (dog) 53–5, 66
Lafayette, Marquis de 42, 43
Lam, Katie 195–6
Lambert, Bill 200
Langworth, Richard 30, 38
Larry (cat) x, 106, 108, 111–13, 115, 135, 145, 149, 150, 151, 155, 160, 165–91, 198–9, 204–206, 209–210, 218, 228, 236, 249, 252, 253
Larry King Live 81
Lassie 240
Lavrov, Sergey 168
Lawn, Connie 89
Lawrence, T. E. 120–21
Lawrence of Abdoun (cat) 120–21
Lawson, Nigel 220–21
leopards 31
Leprechaun (pony) 67

Lessons at 10 programme 161
Lewis, Dana 90
Lewis, Meriwether 42
Liberty (dog) 74–5, 81
Limpert, Jack 78
Lincoln, Abraham 46
Lincoln, Tad 46
Ling-Ling (panda) 247
lions 24, 31–2, 38, 55
Little, Patrick 4–5
Little Beagle Johnson 70
Liukin, Nastia 84
Lloyd George, David 6–7
Lola (dog) 146–8
London Zoo 24, 31–2, 35, 247
Louisiana Purchase 42
Lowe, Rupert 244–5
Lucky (dog) 76–7
Lucy (dog) 221–2

Macaroni (pony) 64, 66, 67
macaws 34, 50, 51
McDonald, Simon 105–110, 112–21
McGraw, Meridith 93
McGuinness, Martin 254
Macintyre, Donald xiv
McKinley, William 49
McLean, Claire 77
Macron, Brigitte 247
Macron, Emmanuel 248
Madam Moose (dog) 41
Maggie (cat) 254–5
Maggie (tortoise) 229
Maine Coons 229
Maisie (cat) 174
Major (dog) 95, 97–8, 99
Major, John xi, 15, 17, 18, 181, 247
Maksat (horse) 247–8
Manchu (dog) 50
Mandelson, Peter xiv
Mao Zedong 247
Margate (cat) 30–31
Marine One 65, 76
Marlon Bundo (rabbit) 95
Martin, Chris 144

Martin, Jill 97
Marybelle (parakeet) 64
Matilda (kangaroo) 24
Maude (pig) 50
May, Theresa 148, 177, 182, 184, 191, 213
Mayhew Animal Home 130–31
Megan (cat) xiii
Menefee, William 44
Menzies, Robert 26
Menzies, Stewart 29
Merkel, Angela 246
mice xii, 46, 105, 111, 117, 133, 145, 154–5,
    172, 204, 217, 230–31
Mike (dog) 63
Miller, Francis 69
Millie (dog) 78, 80
Milner, Gareth 149–50
Ming (panda) 35
Miss Beazley (dog) 84–6
Misty Malarky Ying Yang (cat) 75–6
Mittal, Bharti 201
mockingbirds 42, 49
Mondale, Walter 75
Monroe, Hester Maria 42
Monroe, James 42
Monroe, Marilyn 91
Montague Brown, Anthony 31, 38
Mooly Wooly (cow) 52
Moore, Robbie 189
Mordaunt, Penny 230–31
Mr Protection (possum) 49
Mr Reciprocity (possum) 49
Mullin, Chris 20
Munich Agreement 7, 29
Murdoch, Andy 118–19
Murphy Brown 78
Murray, Ian 186, 252
Murty, Akshata 158–61
musk oxen 247
Mussolini, Benito 36–7

Nandy (dog) 225
National Children's Museum (US) 77
National Dogs in Politics Day 73
National Parks Foundation 82

INDEX

National Zoo, Washington DC 247
Nelson (cat) 25, 28–9
Nemo (cat) 11–12
Newton, Andrew 14–15
Ng, Justin x, 112–13, 172–3, 175–7, 180, 185
Nicholson, Marvin 180–81
Nico (cat) 253
Ninkō, Emperor of Japan 43–4
Nintendo 81
Nixon, Pat 72
Nixon, Richard 71–4, 247, 251
Nixon, Tricia 72, 73
Nixon Eisenhower, Julie 73
Niyazov, Saparmurat 247–8
Noem, Kristi 243–4
Nova (dog) 151, 157–63
Nungaray, Jocelyn 94

Obama, Barack 89–91, 93, 95, 96, 146, 180–81, 242
Obama, Malia 90
Obama, Michelle 90–91
Obama, Sasha 90
Old Abe (eagle) 43
Old Ike (sheep) 52
Old Whiskers (goat) 49
Old Whitey (horse) 45
Oliver, John 95
One Direction 182–3
Orr, Jimmy 83
Osborne, George 145–8
Oscar (dog) 148–9
Oshkosh *aka* Rob Roy (dog) 55, 56
Osmotherly, Edward 124
Ossie (cat) xi, 113–14, 123–32, 150
Ottawa Humane Society 53, 69, 253
Owen, Sid 222
owls 50

Paddy (dog) 12
Paeff, Bashka 55
Pahlavi, Farah 66
Palmer, Patsy 222
Palmerston (cat) x, 107–21, 134, 135, 169, 173–6, 237, 253

Palmerston, Henry John Temple, Viscount 107
Palo Alto 55
panda diplomacy 35–6, 247–9
pandas 35, 247
parakeets 64
Paris Zoo 247
Parke Custis, Nelly 42
Parliament Hill cat sanctuary 253
parrots 42, 44, 49, 229
Parton, Dolly 84
partridges 42
Partygate report 130
Pasha (dog) 73
Patrick (cat) 229
Patterdale terriers 229
Pauline Wayne (cow) 52
peacocks 42
Pebble (dog) 207–208
Pence, Charlotte 95
Pence, Karen 95
Pence, Mike 94–5
People for the Ethical Treatment of Animals (PETA) 92, 209
People's Dispensary for Sick Animals 11
Pepper (dog) 197
Perez, Anna 79
Peta (cat) 11–12
Pete (squirrel) 53
Peter (rabbit) 50
Peter I (cat) 9–10
Peter II (cat) 10
Peter III (cat) 10–11
Peterkin (mouse) 217
pheasants 25, 42
Phelps, Michael 84
pigeons 6, 173, 190
pigs 25, 46, 50, 51
platypuses 35–6
Polaris (cat) 230
Polk, James K. 41
Poll (parrot) 44
pomskies 94
poodles 25, 32–3, 49, 73, 78
Poppy (dog) 151–3, 163

Portuguese water dog 90
possums 49
Powell, Enoch 120
Presidential Pet Museum 77
Prince (cat) 155, 187, 203–205
Prince and Princess of Wales 174
Prudence Prim (dog) 55, 56
Pumpkin (cat) 154–5
Pupniks 66
Puppy Bowl 97
Purr Minister competition 229
Pushinka (dog) 65–6
Putin, Vladimir 85, 246–7

Qing Bao 247
Question Time 224
Quinlan, Lindsey 189–90

rabbits 36, 50, 64, 95, 217
raccoons 51, 56
Ranger (dog) 79–80
Rantzen, Esther 14
rats xii, 51, 105, 124, 165–6
Rayner, Angela 205
Reagan, Ronald 76–8
Reagan, Nancy 76, 77–8
Rebecca (raccoon) 56
Rees, Jonathan 20
Reeves, Rachel 154–5
retrievers 50, 74, 218, 221, 226, 240
Rex (White House dog) 77–8
Rex (Downing Street dog) 148–9
Reynolds, Quentin 28
rhinoceroses 37
Rhodes, Dave 235
Richardson, Ian 213
Ridgway, Claire 3
Rinka (dog) 14–15
Rin Tin Tin (dog) 53
robins 16–17
Robinson, Fraser 90
Rob Roy (horse) 23
Rocco (dog) 108
Romney, Mitt 91–2
Roosevelt, Alice 50, 51

Roosevelt, Charlie 51
Roosevelt, Edith 51
Roosevelt, Eleanor 59
Roosevelt, Franklin Delano 57–9
Roosevelt, Kermit 50
Roosevelt, Quentin 51–2
Roosevelt, Theodore 50–52, 64, 82
roosters 50, 51
Rota (lion) 24, 31–2
Rove, Karl 84, 85
Royal Society for the Prevention of
    Cruelty to Animals (RSPCA) 13, 27
Ruby (dog) 217–18
Ruby Rough (dog) 55
Rufus I (dog) 25, 32–3, 34
Rufus II (dog) 32–4
Ruskell, Mark 251–2
Ryder Cup 85

al-Said, Nuri 31
Sailor Boy (dog) 50
Sansing, John 78
Sardar (horse) 66–7
Sassoon, Philip 26
Saturday Night Live 97–8
Scherzinger, Nicole 183
Scott, Christina 144
Scott, Norman 14–15
Scottish terriers 57–8, 63, 83–7
Seamus (dog) 92
Secret Life of Special Advisers, The xii
Sevier, John 44
Shannon (dog) 67, 68
Sharp, Evelyn 124
Sharp, Owen 230
Sheba (leopard) 31
sheep 52, 64
Short, Martin 98
Siam (cat) 48
Siamese cats 11, 47–8, 74, 75
Siberian cats 204
Sibley, Katherine 79
Sickels, David 47–8
silkworms 44
Simpson, Keith 111

INDEX

Simpsons, The 78
Skinner, Dennis 221
Skip (dog) 50
Slippers (cat) 51
Smith, Curt 79
Smith, Jacqui 144
Smithsonian Museum 55
Smokey, *aka* Rufus of England, *aka* Treasury Bill (cat) 8
Smoky (cat) 29
snakes 37, 50, 52, 95
Snowden, Philip 8
Snowy (dog) 146
Soames, Mary 25
Socks (cat) 18, 81–3
spaniels 42, 63, 68, 71–2, 77–8, 193, 216
Spitting Image 18
Splash (dog) 90
Spot Fletcher (dog) 78
Spunky (dog) 63
squirrels 53
Stafford, Timothy xii
Starmer, Josephine 206
Starmer, Keir x, 123, 130, 153–4, 155, 186, 187, 203–206, 218, 226
Stonewall (dog) 43
Streaker (dog) 66
Strelka (dog) 65
Strictly Come Dancing 183
Stubbs (cat) 236
Sugg, Liz 166–70, 172–5, 180–86, 190–91
Sukey (cow) 44
Sunak, Anoushka 157–8
Sunak, Krishna 157–8
Sunak, Rishi 151, 157–63, 191
Sunny (dog) 91
Susie Gray (cat) 130–31
swans 25, 26, 199–200
Sweet Lips (dog) 41
Swidley, Neil 91
Swire, Hugo 108–109
Sybil (cat) 143–4, 166
Symonds, Carrie 193–7

Taft, Helen 52

Taft, Nellie 52
Taft, William Howard 52
Tango (cat) 28, 32
tarantulas 213–16
Taster (dog) 41
Tatania (cat) 230–31
Tate, Sheila 76
Taurozzi, Danny 253
Taylor, Zachary 45
Ted (dog) 218, 220–21, 223–5
Telesz, Rick 99
Tex (pony) 67
Thatcher, Margaret 13, 77, 224, 229
therapy animals 52–3, 96
Thin Man, The 65
Thomas, Helen 67
Thomson, George 32
Thorpe, Jeremy 14–15
Tiger (cat) 55
tigers 36
TikTok 161
Tiny (cat) xiii
Tiny Tim, *aka* Terrible Tim (dog) 55
Tipler (dog) 41
Tisch Children's Zoo 65
Tits and Tats (cats) 6
Toby (budgerigar) 34–5
Toby (cat) 6
Tom (Chancellor of the Exchequer's cat) 5
Tom (Downing Street cat) 4
Tom Kitten, *aka* Tom Terrific 64
Tomlinson, Louis 182–3
Tommy Liza (cat) 6
Tom Quartz (cat) 50–51
Topsy (cat) 5
tortoises 217, 229
Trillie Williams (cat) 6
True Love (dog) 41
Truman, Bess 63
Truman, Harry 63, 92
Truman, Margaret 63
Trump, Barron 94
Trump, Donald 41, 92–6, 100–101, 193, 205, 236, 241–2, 252

Trump, Ivanka 94
Trump, Lara 94
Trump, Melania 94
Truss, Liz 186, 200
Tugendhat, Tom xi
turkeys 46
Twiss, Jill 95
Twitter x, 91, 109–110, 118–21, 169, 177–9, 235
Twyman, Joe 236–9, 242–3
Tyler, John 44–5

de Valera, Éamon 65, 67
Vallance, Patrick 198
Vance, J. D. 93
Velden, Hanni 18
Vesuvius (horse) 248
Veto (dog) 48–9
Vicky (dog) 73
Vulcan (dog) 41
vultures 37

Wakefield, Mary xiv
Walker, Heather 85
wallabies 55
Washington, George 41–2, 68
Washington, Martha 41–2
Washington Post (parrot) 49
Watters, Edna 254–5
Waugh, Auberon 15
Weimaraners 63–4
Welsh terriers 65, 148–9
Westminster Dog of the Year 152, 230
Westminster Dog Show 109
West Wing, The xiii, 158
White Tips (dog) 66
Whittington, Richard 4
Whitty, Chris 197–8
Whitworth, Marianne 11
Wigg, George 12
Wilberforce (cat) 13–14
Wild Goose Kennels 82
Willetts, David 221
Williams, Bridie 120
Williamson, Gavin 213–16, 238

Williams-Walker, Susan 148–9
Willow (cat) 99, 253
Wilson, Harold 11, 12–13
Wilson, Mary 11–12
Wilson, Woodrow 52–3
Wings 78
Winn-Jones, Lorna 248
Winston (platypus) 36
Winter (dog) 94
Wolff, Isabel 12–13
Wolsey, Thomas 3–4
wolves 37
Wormald, Chris 123
Wright, Oliver 146

Xi Jinping 248
XL bullies 227

Yes, Minister 15
Yes, Prime Minister 15
Yorkshire terriers 73
Yuki (dog) 70–71
Yulin festival 149

Zahawi, Nadhim 129, 150
zebras 51